THE STATE OF MENTAL ILLNESS AND ITS THERAPY

...ATE OF
...ILLNESS
AND ITS THERAPY

Mood Disorders

Joan Esherick

Mason Crest

Mason Crest
450 Parkway Drive, Suite D
Broomall, PA 19008
www.masoncrest.com

Copyright © 2014 by Mason Crest, an imprint of National Highlights, Inc. All rights reserved. No part of this publication may be reproduced or transmitted in any form or by any means, electronic or mechanical, including photocopying, recording, taping or any information storage and retrieval system, without permission from the publisher.

Printed in the Hashemite Kingdom of Jordan.

First printing
9 8 7 6 5 4 3 2 1

Series ISBN: 978-1-4222-2819-7
ISBN: 978-1-4222-2829-6
ebook ISBN: 978-1-4222-8990-7

The Library of Congress has cataloged the
hardcopy format(s) as follows:

Library of Congress Cataloging-in-Publication Data

Esherick, Joan.
 [Drug therapy and mood disorders]
 Mood disorders / Joan Esherick.
   pages cm. – (The state of mental illness and its therapy)
 Audience: Age 12.
 Audience: Grade 7 to 8.
 Revision of: Drug therapy and mood disorders. 2004.
 Includes bibliographical references and index.
 ISBN 978-1-4222-2829-6 (hardcover) – ISBN 978-1-4222-2819-7 (series) – ISBN 978-1-4222-8990-7 (ebook)
 1. Affective disorders–Juvenile literature. 2. Affective disorders–Chemotherapy–Juvenile litera-ture. I. Title.
 RC537.E765 2014
 616.85'27061–dc23
                              2013008199

Produced by Vestal Creative Services.

www.vestalcreative.com

This book is meant to educate and should not be used as an alternative to appropriate medical care. Its cre-ators have made every effort to ensure that the information presented is accurate—but it is not intended to substitute for the help and services of trained professionals.

Picture Credits:
Autumn Libal: p. 53. Benjamin Stewart: p. 66. Comstock: p. 118. Corbis: pp. 76, 110. PhotoDisc: pp. 12, 35, 40, 50, 55, 56, 58, 62, 70, 72, 80. Stockbyte: pp. 10, 14, 15, 46, 48, 68, 84, 89, 92, 98, 106, 108. Wildside: p. 32. The individuals in these images are models, and the images are for illustrative purposes only. To the best knowledge of the publisher, all other images are in the public domain. If any image has been inadvertently uncredited or miscredited, please notify Vestal Creative Services, Vestal, New York 13850, so that rectification can be made for future printings.

CONTENTS

Introduction
by Mary Ann McDonnell

Teenagers have reason to be interested in psychiatric disorders and their treatment. Friends, family members, and even teens themselves may experience one of these disorders. Using scenarios adolescents will understand, this series explains various psychiatric disorders and the drugs that treat them.

Diagnosis and treatment of psychiatric disorders in children between six and eighteen years old are well studied and documented in the scientific journals. A paper appearing in the *Journal of the American Academy of Child and Adolescent Psychiatry* in 2010 estimated that 49.5 percent of all adolescents aged 13 to 18 were affected by at least one psychiatric disorder. Various other studies have reported similar findings. Needless to say, many children and adolescents are suffering from psychiatric disorders and are in need of treatment.

Many children have more than one psychiatric disorder, which complicates their diagnoses and treatment plans. Psychiatric disorders often occur together. For instance, a person with a sleep disorder may also be depressed; a teenager with attention-deficit/hyperactivity disorder (ADHD) may also have a substance-use disorder. In psychiatry, we call this comorbidity. Much research addressing this issue has led to improved diagnosis and treatment.

The most common child and adolescent psychiatric disorders are anxiety disorders, depressive disorders, and ADHD. Sleep disorders, sexual disorders, eating disorders, substance-abuse disorders, and psychotic disorders are also quite common. This series has volumes that address each of these disorders.

Major depressive disorders have been the most commonly diagnosed mood disorders for children and adolescents. Researchers don't agree as to how common mania and bipolar disorder are in children. Some experts believe that manic episodes in children and adolescents are underdiagnosed. Many times, a mood disturbance may co-occur with another psychiatric disorder. For instance, children with ADHD may also be depressed. ADHD is just one psychiatric disorder that is a major health concern for children, adolescents, and adults. Studies of ADHD have reported prevalence rates among children that range from two to 12 percent.

Failure to understand or seek treatment for psychiatric disorders puts children and young adults at risk of developing substance-use disorders. For example, recent research indicates that those with ADHD who were treated with medication were 85 percent less likely to develop a substance-use disorder. Results like these emphasize the importance of timely diagnosis and treatment.

Early diagnosis and treatment may prevent these children from developing further psychological problems. Books like those in this series provide important information, a vital first step toward increased awareness of psychological disorders; knowledge and understanding can shed light on even the most difficult subject. These books should never, however, be viewed as a substitute for professional consultation. Psychiatric testing and an evaluation by a licensed professional are recommended to determine the needs of the child or adolescent and to establish an appropriate treatment plan.

Foreword
by Donald Esherick

We live in a society filled with technology—from computers surfing the Internet to automobiles operating on gas and batteries. In the midst of this advanced society, diseases, illnesses, and medical conditions are treated and often cured with the administration of drugs, many of which were unknown thirty years ago. In the United States, we are fortunate to have an agency, the Food and Drug Administration (FDA), which monitors the development of new drugs and then determines whether the new drugs are safe and effective for use in human beings.

When a new drug is developed, a pharmaceutical company usually intends that drug to treat a single disease or family of diseases. The FDA reviews the company's research to determine if the drug is safe for use in the population at large and if it effectively treats the targeted illnesses. When the FDA finds that the drug is safe and effective, it approves the drug for treating that specific disease or condition. This is called the labeled indication.

During the routine use of the drug, the pharmaceutical company and physicians often observe that a drug treats other medical conditions besides what is indicated in the labeling. Studies may be conducted to further demonstrate the drug's effectiveness in these conditions, but the results may not be conclusive. While the labeling will not include the treatment of the particular condition, a physician can still prescribe the drug to a patient with this disease. This is known as an unlabeled or off-label indication.

I have reviewed the books in this series from the perspective of the pharmaceutical industry and the FDA, specifically focusing on the labeled indications, uses, and known side effects of these drugs. Further information can be found on the FDA's website (www.FDA. gov).

Depression is just one form of mood disorder.

Chapter One

Defining Mood Disorders

t would be so easy, Todd thought as he turned his father's hunting shotgun over again and again in his hands. *It could all be finished, just like that. No more pain. No more pressure. No more letting everyone else down.*

"Todd?" his mother called from upstairs, interrupting his thoughts. "Todd? Are you down there? Did you put your dad's hunting gear away yet?"

"Yeah, Mom." Todd sighed. He paused to take a last look at what he thought might deliver him from his anguish, then put the twelve-gauge shotgun into his father's gun cabinet. *If only it had been loaded.*

An "Eeyore attitude" toward life may be a symptom of a mood disorder.

Seventeen-year-old Todd had once been an energetic, easygoing kid—the kind that loved life and that most other kids wanted to be around. His friends enjoyed his goofy sense of humor; his classmates laughed at his jokes; his teachers admired how well he juggled schoolwork, a part-time job, and his responsibilities as the swim team captain. Todd remembered well his old self, and his old life. But that was done now. Life wasn't the same. He wasn't the same. And he never would be again. Not since leukemia took his nine-year-old sister.

Since Megan died, Todd felt like he lived in a bubble of looming darkness. He expected to be sad at first, but he didn't think he'd hurt this much for this long. Nothing gave him pleasure anymore. Nothing mattered. When he wasn't tired or feeling worthless and guilty, he was angry.

How can they go on like nothing's happened? Todd's rage pounded in his brain. *How can they live like she was never here? God, how could you let her die? Meg, why did you have to leave?* Todd didn't know what to think anymore. He just wanted the pain to end.

Unlike Todd, fifteen-year-old Sharon can't remember a time when she felt happy or excited. She'd never been peppy or upbeat about anything. Life always felt like a giant "sigh." Nothing more, nothing less. Even as a young child she remembers kids teasing her and calling her "Eeyore," because her gloomy disposition seemed so much like that of the sad character from A. A. Milne's Winnie the Pooh stories. If normal life were painted in brilliant reds, yellows, blues, and greens, her life would be painted in one ho-hum shade of gray.

Sharon's chronic "blah" attitude isolated her from other teens her age. No one hung with "Eeyore-girl." No one wanted her at parties. Sharon spent most of her time alone in her room: sometimes crying, sometimes reading, sometimes sleeping to avoid her loneliness. And sometimes she just stared off into space while thoughts swirled through her foggy brain.

Will it ever get any better than this? Is this all there is? Why can't I just be happy like everyone else?

And then there's Regina. A highly motivated, overachieving high school senior, Regina is full of self-confidence and boundless energy. As editor of the school newspaper, she thrives on the thrill of setting and meeting deadlines, whether for her own or others' writing assignments. But sometimes her feelings of confidence get carried away. Sometimes she's too happy. When feeling particularly "high," Regina is convinced she can do *anything*, so she'll take on unrealistic assignments or assume deadlines that are impossible to meet.

During these upbeat mood swings, Regina behaves impulsively. She may walk up to a stranger at the gas station, start talking, and

A person with a bipolar disorder may enjoy the "highs"—but the "lows" are far less fun!

All of us experience emotional ups and downs.

not be able to stop. She may get some new idea for the school news-paper in the middle of the night and call her sleeping coeditors to tell them her ideas—even if it's three o'clock in the morning! Nor-mally comfortable and casual in the style of clothes she wears, when Regina's in this kind of mood she wears sleek, seductive clothes. The possibility of having sex with a stranger seems fun and exhilarating to Regina; she doesn't care about the consequences.

When Regina is "up," she sometimes goes on spending sprees at the local mall, running up thousands of dollars on her father's credit cards. She buys gifts for her coeditors, reporters, and photographers without any thought to cost. She sometimes tells others that that she is a personal acquaintance of her favorite rock star and that she is shopping for him.

Regina looks forward to her highs. She feels exhilarated and alive when her on-top-of-the-world mood kicks in. The deep downward spiral she inevitably experiences when the high finally passes—the "crash" she so dreads but that always comes—is a small price to pay for the thrill of feeling invincible and carefree.

Todd, Sharon, and Regina are three teens with three very different problems. Have you ever felt like they felt? Do you know anyone like them? Though their circumstances differ, they share something in common: Each suffers from a mood disorder.

What are Mood Disorders?

We all experience "the blues" now and then, those brief times when we feel "down" or "depressed." We all enjoy moments of happiness and well-being, too. Teens, especially, go through emotional highs and lows. But for someone with a mood disorder, these changes in mood go well beyond normal. When a person's moods (whether up or down) become extreme enough to keep that person from doing his normal tasks at home, at school, or at work, or if they cause a person to consider harming herself or others, doctors will suspect a mood disorder.

A mood disorder is a condition rooted in the brain that causes disturbances in the way a person thinks, feels, or acts, but especially affects the person's moods. That effect can go in either direction: the person may experience good moods that are "too good" or bad moods that are "too bad." Some mood disorders involve swings back and forth between both good and bad. You've probably heard words like "clinical depression," "manic depression," "mild depression," or "seasonal depression." These are common terms people use to describe mood disorders.

Mood disorders are more common than we think. The U.S. Centers for Disease Control and Prevention (the CDC) estimate that almost one in ten people suffer from depression each year. The National Youth Network suggests that seven to 14 percent of American children will experience at least one episode of major depression by the time they reach age fifteen. That's roughly one out of every ten kids! The American Academy of Child and Adolescent Psychiatry tells us that at any given moment, one in twenty children is depressed. And children in the United States aren't alone in their struggle. According to the World Health Organization, depression is the leading cause of disability in the world.

Q & A

Question: How can I know if I'm at risk for developing a mood disorder?

Answer: While the exact cause of mood disorders remains somewhat unclear, certain factors can make you more or less likely to develop one:

- Family history: If a close relative (parent, sibling, grandparent, etc.) has (or had) a mood disorder, you are at greater risk for developing one, too. Mood disorders often run in families.
- Genetics: Genes can cause many diseases or can influence the severity of a disease. In people with mood disorders, scientists observe that interactions between certain genes can produce a susceptibility to the disorder.
- Physical health: If you have a medical condition or other psychological disorders, if you take prescription medication, are in overall poor health, don't exercise, and don't maintain a balanced diet, you have a higher risk of getting mood disorders.
- Stress level: Everyone experiences stress, but too much stress (too many commitments, family problems, relationship troubles, job or school pressure) can increase your risk of developing a mood disorder.
- Significant loss or traumatic life events: Has a loved one recently died? Did you just move out of state and leave your friends behind? Major life changes can greatly increase your risk of becoming depressed.

Five Mood Disorder Myths and the Facts to Correct Them

1. MYTH: Teens don't suffer from depression; they're just moody.
   FACT: Depression occurs in people of any age, gender, race, socioeconomic group, or geographic location.
2. MYTH: Most depressed people are able to "snap out of it."
   FACT: Depression and other mood disorders will not just go away; in many cases, they have a biochemical cause. Young people and adults alike need professional treatment in order to overcome mood disorders.
3. MYTH: Medications for mood disorders are crutches for weak people.
   FACT: Most mood disorders are medical problems rooted in the biology of the brain. Willpower alone cannot cure these disorders. It takes great character strength to admit you need help.
4. MYTH: People with severe mood disorders can't be treated effectively.
   FACT: Eighty to 90 percent of people with depression and bipolar disorder find successful medical treatment for their disorders.
5. MYTH: Mood disorders are quickly and easily diagnosed.
   FACT: Canada's Centre for Addiction and Mental Health (CAMH) cites that nearly 30 percent of patients with mood disorders surveyed reported that it took over ten years to receive a correct diagnosis. Over 60 percent said they had received an incorrect diagnosis before receiving the correct one.

Using the DSM-IV-TR

The DSM-IV-TR based its lists of possible diagnoses on two research criteria, which reflect major aspects of scientific study:

- validity (Are these real disorders?)
- reliability (Do different psychiatrists and other medical practitioners seeing the same patient make the same diagnosis?)

Diagnosing Mood Disorders

Mood disorders come in many shapes and sizes; so many, in fact, that psychiatrists use a special book called the *Diagnostic and Statistical Manual of Mental Disorders* (currently the fourth edition, text revision—the DSM-IV-TR) to guide them in determining which disorder a patient has. Because mood disorders can present themselves in several ways (changes in mood, thinking ability, physical health, and behavior), the DSM-IV-TR lists specific criteria for each type of mood disorder based on how the patient thinks, acts, and feels. If a patient's symptoms match the criteria, the doctor can say his patient has that specific disorder.

criteria: Characteristics on which a decision or diagnosis may be based.

This is a little like using a manual to "diagnose" various types of sports. Let's say you are learning about American sports and you observe a sporting event. As you watch the game, you notice these things: players use a round orange ball; they play on a rectangular court; the court has two circular rims with nets attached suspended above the court at each end; players bounce the ball with one hand most of the time, but sometimes throw the ball to each other or through the suspended hoop. You may be somewhat familiar with American sports, but just to be sure it isn't another sport, you check your manual. Sure enough, under the heading "Basketball" you see the following traits listed: orange ball; rectangular court; passing between players; goal is to throw ball through hoop, and so on. By comparing what you observe with the description listed in your manual, you make your diagnosis. This sporting event is a basketball game.

diagnosis: The medical opinion reached after identifying the nature and cause of a patient's disease or injury. A diagnosis is reached by examining the patient, the patient's history, and the patient's medical test results.

array: An ordered list.

Doctors and other medical practitioners use a similar process to diagnose mood disorders. But identifying mood disorders is more complicated than diagnosing sporting events. Patients with mood disorders present an array of symptoms, many of which look like other illnesses or can be present in several different kinds of mood disorders. Medical practitioners need to know which symptoms go with which disorders to be able to tell the disorders apart. That's what the DSM-IV-TR does for them.

The DSM-IV-TR provides a complete listing of specific symptoms and their combinations for each disorder. The practitioner observes a patient, and if a patient's symptoms match the symptoms listed for

DSM-IV-TR Criteria for Major Depressive Episode

To be diagnosed with Major Depressive Episode, you must have experienced the following for two weeks or more:

A depressed mood (feeling sad or empty) for most of the day, nearly every day

AND/OR

A loss of interest or pleasure in nearly all things you used to enjoy,

PLUS

Any four of these symptoms:

- Gaining weight or losing weight (when not dieting)
- Being unable to sleep nearly every day
- Experiencing changes in speed of body movement, which is noticed by others
- Feeling tired all the time or like you have less energy
- Feeling worthless or excessively guilty
- Being less able to think clearly, concentrate, or make decisions
- Thinking about death, suicide (with or without a plan), or making a suicide attempt

To be a major depressive episode, all of the above cannot be caused by another illness or drug use/abuse, cannot be part of a mixed episode, and cannot be explained as the normal grief a person experiences after the loss of a loved one.

Mood Disorder Diagnostic Criteria At-a-Glance

Type of Disorder	How long has the patient experienced symptoms?	Which types of episodes has the patient had? How many?	Does the patient have other symptoms of depression?
Depressive Disorders:			
major depressive disorder	two weeks minimum	At least one major depressive episode, but NO manic, mixed, or hypomanic episodes	yes, at least four
dysthymic disorder	two years minimum	none	yes, but not severe enough to be called major depressive episode
Bipolar Disorders:			
Bipolar I	average of four episodes over ten years	one or more manic or mixed episodes, usually accompanied by major depressive episodes	those consistent with major depressive episodes
Bipolar II	higher number of episodes, as many as four per year	one or more major depressive episodes accompanied by at least one hypomanic episode, but NO manic or mixed episodes	those consistent with major depressive episodes

Mood Disorder Diagnostic Criteria At-a-Glance

cyclothymic disorder	two years minimum	none	yes, hypomanic and depressive symptoms, but not severe enough to be called hypomanic or major depressive episodes

a particular disorder in the DSM-IV-TR, the doctor or other practitioner can say which disorder the patient has.

What kinds of things are listed in the DSM-IV-TR? What symptoms do doctors observe? To learn how psychiatrists or other mental health workers diagnose mood disorders, we need to understand what kinds of symptoms they look for in a patient. One criterion is whether or not the patient has experienced certain kinds of "episodes" as they are described in the DSM-IV-TR. The DSM-IV-TR lists four kinds of episodes doctors can look for in a patient.

Major Depressive Episode

When a patient feels really "down" *for at least two weeks* (or doesn't enjoy activities he used to enjoy), and experiences at least four more symptoms of depression (see page 21), psychiatrists say that he has experienced a Major Depressive Episode. The patient's depressed mood (his feeling "down") during this time must be unrelated to other illnesses or drug use/abuse and may include feelings of sadness, hopelessness, discouragement, or worthlessness, or extreme irritability.

If a patient's symptoms match the symptoms listed under Major Depressive Episode, then the doctor knows that the patient has experienced that kind of episode.

Manic Episode

A patient has had a manic episode when she has experienced at least one week of unusually and consistently elevated or agitated mood ("on a high") while exhibiting three of these additional symptoms:

- having an inflated ego or feelings of great self-importance;
- needing less sleep;
- needing to talk more and faster than usual;
- having thoughts and ideas constantly racing in her mind;
- becoming too easily distracted, even by small things;
- getting more done in school, at work, and in other goal-driven activities than she could before;
- pursuing intensely pleasurable activities even when they will likely result in painful consequences (shopping sprees, impulsive sex, foolish decisions, high-risk or dangerous activities).

To be labeled a manic episode, the high described above cannot be part of a mixed episode (see below), must not result from drug use or abuse, and must be extreme enough to severely impact the person's ability to work, go to school, maintain relationships, or function normally.

euphoric: Having an exaggerated feeling of happiness or well-being.

Mixed Episode

When a person has all the symptoms necessary to be diagnosed with both a manic episode *and* a major depressive episode (except how long it lasts) nearly every day for at least one week, doctors say that person has had a mixed episode. This feels like a roller-coaster ride of emotional ups and downs.

Additional Symptoms of Depression

(beyond depressed mood or loss of interest in things previously enjoyed)

- Weight loss
- Weight gain
- Difficulty sleeping or sleeping too much
- Body movements and speech either speeded up or slowed down
- Loss of energy or feeling constantly tired
- Feeling worthless, self-critical, or inappropriately guilty
- Feeling hopeless
- Difficulty thinking clearly or concentrating
- Difficulty making decisions
- Thinking about suicide

Hypomanic Episode

When someone experiences a sudden, euphoric, cheerful high lasting at least four days that has the same symptoms as a manic episode but isn't extreme enough to cause severe problems in the patient's ability to take care of normal responsibilities, she is probably experiencing a hypomanic episode.

A doctor's first step in diagnosing a mood disorder is to determine if the patient has experienced any of the episodes described above. But her diagnosis is not yet complete. Now, using what she's learned about her patient's episodes, she has to identify the specific disorder.

Mood Disorders in Common Terms

Major depression: Also called "clinical depression," this disorder is characterized by a severely depressed mood that occurs with additional symptoms (lack of energy, sleep problems, appetite problems, problems in concentration, etc.), that lasts two weeks or more, and that interferes with the person's ability to function normally.

Manic depression: Technically called "bipolar disorder," this mood disorder has alternating cycles of extreme emotional ups and downs.

Mild depression: This long-lasting depression (two to five years) is technically called "dysthymia" and includes symptoms that are mild enough that the person can still go to school and work, but that still cause the person to be chronically sad and pessimistic.

Postpartum depression: Also known as the "baby blues," this form of depression happens after a woman gives birth, and it is believed to be caused by changing hormone levels.

Seasonal depression: This mood disorder, also known as "seasonal affective disorder" or "winter depression," causes a person to be depressed in the winter (primarily) when daylight hours are the shortest. Spring and increased daylight bring relief.

Types of Mood Disorders

After the practitioner identifies which episodes the patient has experienced, he can refer to the DSM-IV-TR again to determine which mood disorder is involved. The DSM-IV-TR divides mood disorders into four basic categories.

Depressive Disorders

Depressive disorders include those mood disorders that involve a depressed state of mind (feeling "low" or "blah") or chronic sadness but that *are not* accompanied by times of feeling "up" or "high." We commonly call these disorders "depression." The DSM-IV-TR identifies three major types of depressive disorders based on how severe the symptoms are and how long they last.

Major Depressive Disorder
This disorder is also sometimes called "major depression," "clinical depression," or "unipolar depression." It is marked by symptoms that include at least one major depressive episode and at least four additional symptoms of depression (see below).

Our fictional character, Todd, who opened this chapter, struggled with a major depressive disorder that was triggered by the death of his sister a year ago.

Dysthymic Disorder
Sometimes called "chronic depression" or "mild depression," this disorder is suspected in people who experience at least two years of a depressed mood (with more bad days than good overall) but do not have enough other symptoms to qualify as a major depressive episode or disorder.

Though she thought her personality was to blame, "Eeyore girl" Sharon's down-in-the-dumps moods weren't a result of her personality at all; she had dysthymic disorder.

Drug Approval

Before a drug can be marketed in the United States, it must be officially approved by the Food and Drug Administration (FDA). Today's FDA is the primary consumer protection agency in the United States. Operating under the authority given it by the government, and guided by laws established throughout the twentieth century, the FDA has established a rigorous drug approval process that verifies the safety, effectiveness, and accuracy of labeling for any drug marketed in the United States.

While the United States has the FDA for the approval and regulation of drugs and medical devices, Canada has a similar organization called the Therapeutic Product Directorate (TPD). The TPD is a division of Health Canada, the Canadian government department of health. The TPD regulates drugs, medical devices, disinfectants, and sanitizers with disinfectant claims. Some of the things that the TPD monitors are quality, effectiveness, and safety. Just as the FDA must approve new drugs in the United States, the TPD must approve new drugs in Canada before those drugs can enter the market.

Depressive Disorder Not Otherwise Specified
This includes other types of depression that do not exhibit enough symptoms to be called a major depressive disorder, dysthymic disorder, or other related depressive disorders, but are depression nonetheless. This is a kind of catchall category for depressions that don't match all the symptoms listed in the other categories.

Bipolar Disorders

Unlike depressive disorders, bipolar disorders (formerly called "manic depression") include alternating lows and highs. A person with a bipolar disorder can swing from feeling sluggish, worthless, and blue to feeling revved up, invincible, and on top of the world over the course of hours, days, weeks, and months. The DSM-IV-TR lists four types of bipolar disorders.

Bipolar I

This form of bipolar disorder involves at least one manic or mixed episode as well as one major depressive episode. Both must be present for the patient to have Bipolar I. Because Bipolar I tends to be recurrent, people with this disorder experience more than one episode in their lifetime.

School newspaper editor Regina's intense highs were typical of the manic phase of a bipolar disorder. Her doctor later diagnosed her as having Bipolar I.

Bipolar II

For a diagnosis of Bipolar II, a patient must have experienced at least one (or more) major depressive episode(s) and one (or more) hypomanic episode(s), but not have experienced manic or mixed episodes. If the patient has manic or mixed episodes, he does not have Bipolar II. This disorder usually starts down in mood but is accompanied by at least one hypomanic phase.

Cyclothymic Disorder

The DSM-IV-TR states that this category of bipolar disorder includes at least two years of alternating manic and depressive symptoms. A patient with cyclothymic disorder suffers from constant mood swings, but her moods aren't severe enough to be called major depressive or manic episodes—and yet they are difficult enough to disrupt her life.

Bipolar Disorder Not Otherwise Specified

Sometimes a patient has manic-depressive symptoms, but the symptoms don't fit any other bipolar category. His symptoms may not last long enough or may include a manic episode without depression. He may have "ups" without "downs," or his symptoms may not be severe. If the doctor feels a bipolar condition exists but she can't match the patient's symptoms to the criteria for other bipolar disorders, she will categorize it here.

Mood Disorder Due to a General Medical Condition

In addition to depressive and bipolar disorders, patients can have mood disorders that result from other illnesses or injuries, such as a brain tumor, stroke, underactive thyroid, or multiple sclerosis. If the patient's mood disorder can be traced to a disease, illness, or injury, it is not considered a depressive or bipolar disorder. It is identified as being due to a medical condition.

Substance-Induced Mood Disorder

Sometimes mood disorders don't come from illnesses or medical conditions; they are linked instead to side effects of medication or the result of taking or abusing other drugs. When the origin of a patient's mood disorder can be traced to drugs or other substances he has taken or been exposed to, the patient is said to have substance-induced mood disorder.

Mood disorders can be difficult to diagnose, particularly because there are no cut-and-dry, measurable tests you can take to diagnose a mood disorder. If, for example, a doctor suspects you have asthma, he can do a lung function study to see how well your lungs process oxygen when you exercise. If he suspects you have diabetes, he can measure your blood sugar levels by doing a blood test. If he thinks you might have a broken bone in your foot, he can order an X-ray. But doctors don't have these kinds of tests for mood disorders; you can't take a blood test or have an X-ray done to diagnose depression. That's why the DSM-IV-TR is so important. Medical practitioners rely on the information provided in this manual (as well as their research and clinical experience) to help them understand, diagnose, and treat psychological disorders.

Once a doctor makes her diagnosis, she is ready to develop a treatment plan with her patient. Treatments, which we will look at in chapters four and seven, can include both drug and non-drug strategies. While counselors, psychologists, therapists, and clergy can provide nondrug therapies to complement drug treatments, only medical doctors and advanced care nurses can prescribe medications to treat mood disorders.

Abraham Lincoln is just one historical figure who may have experienced a mood disorder.

Chapter Two

The History and Development of Mood Disorder Drugs

magine being asked to a banquet. "Only a select few are invited," the invitation reads, but it of course does not include a guest list. You feel honored and decide to attend, but who else will be there?

On the big night you wash your car, put on your rented tuxedo (or gown), and drive to the reception hall. With sweaty palms and a racing heart, you approach the facility. You can't help but notice the long line of limousines and Lincolns emptying their dignitaries onto the red-carpeted sidewalk outside. If you didn't know better, you'd think you'd been invited to Hollywood's Oscars.

You park your car and make your way to the dining room. There, on one of the linen-covered round tables toward the front, you see your name on a place card. Yes, that's your name, and yes, the invitation was meant for you, but as you look around, you wonder how you could've been included among this group of guests: Mark Twain, Abraham Lincoln, Vincent van Gogh, Teddy Roosevelt, Ludwig van Beethoven, Edgar Allen Poe, Winston Churchill, Charles Schultz, Richard Nixon, Buzz Aldrin, Ty Cobb, Tipper Gore, Anthony Hopkins, Dwight Gooden, Elton John, Rosie O'Donnell, Darryl Strawberry, Mike Wallace—the list could go on and on. Athletes, actors, astronauts, painters, poets, presidents—you name it, they're there! What could you possibly have in common with these famous people?

You've probably guessed by now that this banquet was held for a special members-only club—but you might be surprised to learn that the club consists of those having a mood disorder. As recorded and confirmed in their biographies, autobiographies, personal writings, interviews, documentaries, or other historical documents, the historical figures and famous people listed experienced a mood disorder at some time during their lives. If you have a mood disorder, you have something in common with these legends. You're in good company.

Mood disorders (as you can tell from the banquet guest list) have been around for a long time—centuries, in fact. Only since the mid-twentieth century have drug treatments for mood disorders been consistently and effectively used. This doesn't mean that drug treatments weren't tried; physicians in the early first and second centuries treated their patients with chemicals, though they were unaware they were doing so. They told their patients to take baths in certain types of natural water sources. We now know that these waters contained naturally occurring chemicals, but physicians then

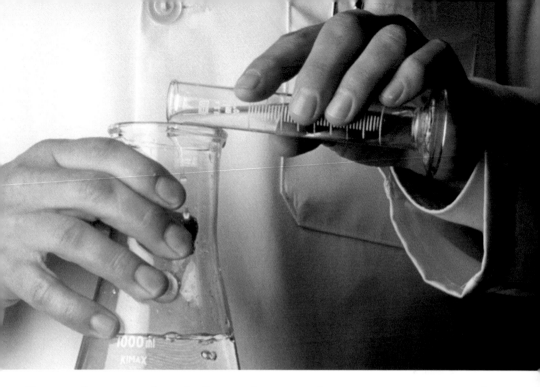

Researchers use chemical samples to explore ways to treat mood disorders.

didn't know that; they only knew that these special waters helped their patients.

Early Treatments

According to Dr. Alvin Silverstein's work *Depression* (coauthored with his wife, Virginia Silverstein and their daughter Laura Silverstein Nunn), a man named Soranus of Ephesus, a second-century Greek physician, treated depression and manic-depression with mineral waters, which contained lithium, the chemical used today to treat bipolar disorder. Another Greek physician encouraged his manic patients to bathe in alkaline springs, which also, in all likelihood, contained lithium. Did these first-millennium physicians know that lithium was the curative property in these waters? No, the element

Quote from Florence Nightingale (Who Suffered from Depression)

O weary day, O evenings that never end! For how many long years I have watched that drawing-room clock and thought it would never reach the ten! . . . In my thirty-first year I see nothing desirable but death.

Florence Nightingale wrote this in 1850, four years before becoming the champion of wounded soldiers during the Crimean War. Today, because of reforms she caused in the treatment of the sick and injured and because of her insistence on sanitary conditions and proper hygiene, this once-depressed hero is considered the mother of modern nursing.

lithium (an alkaline metal) wasn't discovered until the early 1800s, but these intuitive practitioners knew that something contained within the waters improved their patients' symptoms.

Like their Roman counterparts, European doctors of the nineteenth and early-twentieth centuries prescribed mineral baths for patients with mood disorders. By this time, physicians knew of the presence of lithium and other chemicals in the healing pools, but though the waters eased their patients' troubled spirits, the doctors could not pinpoint the exact chemical in the water that cured their patients' ills.

It wasn't until the mid-twentieth century, just fifty years ago, that specific drugs began to be identified as treatment options for people with mood dis-

psychotherapy: Various forms of psychological treatment involving counselors, therapists, and other mental health workers. Often includes "talk" therapies.

Classes of Antidepressants Discovered Since 1949

Mood Stabilizers (lithium)
Monoamine Oxidase Inhibitors (MAOIs)
Tricyclic Antidepressants (TCAs)
Selective Serotonin Reuptake Inhibitors (SSRIs)

orders. Until these discoveries were made, doctors considered the most effective treatments for depressed patients to be psychotherapy and electroconvulsive therapy (ECT).

In the 1950s, ECT was as horrific as its name implies. The patient was strapped to a table and several electrodes were attached to select locations on the person's head. A technician threw a switch, and electrical currents traveled through the electrodes into the person's brain, causing massive seizures. To keep the patient from biting his tongue—and to muffle his screams of pain—doctors routinely wedged something into the patient's mouth. The treatment, though barbaric, seemed to work. Seizure activity in the brain improved symptoms in people with severe mood disorders.

electroconvulsive therapy (ECT): Treatment for psychiatric disorders that involves sending electrical current through the patient's brain.

seizures: A sudden attack that may include loss of motor ability.

Thankfully for the psychiatric patient, the late 1940s and 1950s became an age of discovery regarding new drug treatments for people with mood disorders.

First Drug Discoveries

The first breakthrough discovery for that era came from "down under." Australian physician John Frederick Joseph Cade believed that some kind of toxin must be causing his manic patients' bizarre behaviors. To test his hypothesis, historians tell us that Dr. Cade took urine samples from each of his patients to see if he could detect the presence of an abnormal toxin. He suspected that the toxin might be similar to uric acid, which occurs naturally when the body processes proteins and is disposed of through the body's urine. Dr. Cade needed uric acid samples to compare with his patients' urine samples to see if any unusual toxins were present. To make uric acid, he used a form of the chemical that dissolved easily in water. That form contained lithium.

Dr. Cade first tested his manufactured sample on laboratory animals to make sure it was harmless. When he tested his lithium urate on the normally high-strung guinea pigs, it didn't hurt them, but the rodents became very calm. He wanted to try the compound on his manic patients, but he wasn't sure if the drug was safe for humans. After not being able to convince his research assistants to try the drug, he tried it on himself! And he lived to tell the tale.

Knowing the drug was safe for human consumption, he tested it on his patients, and more than 80 percent experienced improvement in their manic symptoms. Lithium had the same calming effect on human beings as it had on lab animals.

His results were very promising, but lithium is toxic for human beings if given at high doses. Several patients undergoing lithium treatment died. Because of the difficulty in making lithium safe for humans, the U.S. Food and Drug Administration (FDA), America's regulatory agency that oversees the manufacture and sale of drugs, did not approve lithium for use in people with bipolar disorder until the early 1970s. Since then it has become the drug of choice for people with bipolar disorders.

Though the Australian doctor's work didn't result in a treatment for bipolar disorder until twenty years later, his research revealed

Key Developments in the History of Mood Disorder Drug Treatment

1817: Lithium is discovered by Johann A. Arfvedson.

1949: Australian doctor John Cade observes a lithium compound's calming effect in guinea pigs, tries the drug on himself, and begins treating patients with manic symptoms with the drug. Lithium works.

1952: French surgeon Henri Laborit, while trying to discover a way to reduce postoperative shock in surgical patients, discovers that chlorpromazine, which when given to his patients, not only reduces their postsurgical complications but also results in psychological benefits.

1953: Doctors notice that the tuberculosis drug, iproniazid, improves TB patients' mood and energy levels. Research is started to probe the possible effectiveness of iproniazid in depressed patients who did not have TB.

1954: The FDA approves chlorpromazine for use in psychiatric patients in the United States. By 1964, fifty million patients worldwide are taking the drug.

1957: Results of the hugely successful iproniazid study are released. Iproniazid becomes the first modern antidepressant.

1957–1958: Over four hundred thousand depressed patients are treated with iproniazid.

1958: Imipramine, the first tricyclic antidepressant is released. Amitriptyline follows.

1970: U.S. FDA approves lithium for use in treating mania.

1974: U.S. FDA approves lithium as a preventative treatment for bipolar disorders.

1987: U.S. FDA approves Prozac, the first SSRI, for use in treating depression.

a chemical component to the treatment of people with mood disorders. Talk therapy and electric shock treatment weren't the only possible source of help for psychiatric symptoms: Dr. Cade's research opened the door to treating psychiatric patients with drugs.

He wasn't the only doctor to make such discoveries. In 1952, just three years after Dr. Cade's groundbreaking discovery, a French surgeon, Henri Laborit, was making headway in research of his own.

Accidental Discoveries

Dr. Laborit was looking for a way to reduce complications, especially a drop in blood pressure, that many of his patients faced when they

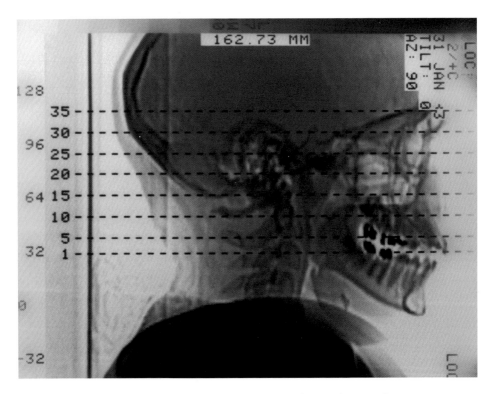

X-rays can only provide limited clues about brain function. Researchers use other techniques to help them understand the action of various brain chemicals.

were recovering from surgery. The anesthesia he used to put his patients to sleep during their operations was the primary cause of his patients' postoperative shock. If the surgeon could reduce the amount of anesthesia he had to use on patients during an operation, he might reduce their amount of shock. He also knew that certain brain chemicals caused shock, so if he could find other chemicals to counteract the shock-causing chemicals, his patients would experience less of this postoperative complication. He tried allergy medications called antihistamines.

postoperative: After surgery.

Surprisingly, when Dr. Laborit gave large doses of anti-allergy drugs to his surgical patients, they seemed calmer before surgery. They didn't seem concerned about what they were about to undergo; they weren't even nervous. Most patients saw the greatest calming result from a drug called chlorpromazine. When Dr. Laborit communicated his results to another surgeon, that surgeon told his psychiatrist brother-in-law, Pierre Deniker, who decided to try Dr. Laborit's method of calming his surgical patients on his own agitated psychiatric patients. The results were amazing. Like the surgical patients, Dr. Deniker's patients calmed down.

While these doctors were discovering a connection between drugs and psychological behavior, a pharmaceutical company in the United States purchased the ownership and manufacturing rights to the very drug that had produced such promising results for the two French physicians: chlorpromazine. The FDA approved chlorpromazine for use in the United States in 1954, and the drug's calming effects were immediately apparent in American psychiatric patients. Many uncontrollable patients who had once been warehoused in psychiatric hospitals could now lead nearly normal lives.

When discussing the haphazard way in which chlorpromazine came to be used for psychiatric disorders, Nancy Andreasen, a leading researcher in the field of mental illness, notes, "The first powerful drug available to treat serious mental illness was discovered in

Brand Names vs. Generic Names

Talking about psychiatric drugs can be confusing, because every drug has at least two names: its "generic name" and the "brand name" that the pharmaceutical company uses to market the drug. Generic names come from the drugs' chemical structures, while drug companies use brand names in order to inspire public recognition and loyalty for their products.

much the same way as penicillin: by accident."

But there was still one more accidental discovery to come that would permanently change the way mood disorders were treated.

True Antidepressants Are Born

In 1953, a serious lung disease called tuberculosis (TB) was claiming the lives of 50 percent of its victims: for every two people who contracted the disease, one would die if left untreated. Before the development of antibiotics later in the decade, which effectively wiped out TB in the United States, another drug, iproniazid, was the number-one weapon against this deadly disease.

Though iproniazid was designed to treat TB, which it did, doctors noticed an added benefit to the drug. When they administered it to TB patients, the patients' energy levels went up, their appetites increased, and their overall feelings of happiness and well-being greatly improved. This drug, designed to treat a deadly lung infection, resulted in positive emotional and psychological outcomes.

Researchers and psychiatrists took notice and began testing the iproniazid in depressed patients. In 1957, these doctors reported their findings: iproniazid was consistently successful in treating depression. Within a year, doctors prescribed the new antidepressant drug for more than 400,000 patients who suffered from depression. Nearly all responded favorably to the treatment. Doctors finally had a drug in their arsenal for fighting depression, even though they still didn't understand how it worked.

Researchers later discovered that iproniazid stopped a certain enzyme in the brain (called monoamine oxidase) from destroying certain other brain chemicals that affect mood. Because of how it worked in the brain, iproniazid was considered the first monoamine oxidase inhibitor (MAOI), a type of antidepressant still in use today. (To learn more about types of antidepressants and how they work, see chapter three.)

Unfortunately, iproniazid's success didn't last long; it had to be pulled off the market shortly after its widespread debut because of toxic side effects. Though its time on the market was brief, iproniazid demonstrated that drugs, without additional therapies, could help depression. This discovery paved the way for the rapid development of additional antidepressant medications.

debut: First appearance.

tricyclic antidepressants [TCAs]: Type of antidepressant used to treat mood disorders.

By the end of the 1950s, doctors were using imipramine hydrochloride (Tofanil) and amitriptyline hydrochloride (Elavil), the first of the tricyclic antidepressants [TCAs] to treat depressed patients all over the United States.

For the next thirty years, drug treatment for depression relied almost exclusively on these two classes of antidepressant drugs (MAOIs and TCAs). These types of drugs, however, while they worked well in treating depression, caused unpleasant side effects: dry mouth, intestinal discomfort (especially constipation), increased or rapid heart rate, and excessive drowsiness. Doctors felt that MAOIs and TCAs didn't just affect one chemical in the brain, but many. The drugs worked generally all over the brain, causing the unwanted side effects. Researchers hoped to discover a new kind of drug that would target only one chemical or one part of the brain but still be effective in treating depression, too.

A New Class of Antidepressant

In the early 1970s, David Wong, a researcher at pharmaceutical firm Eli Lilly and Company, tried a new research technique that allowed him to see how nerve cells in rat brains interacted with other brain chemicals. He observed firsthand how certain drugs had a more general effect on the brain and how others targeted specific chemicals. If only they could find a drug that acted on only one chemical in the brain!

By 1976, Wong and fellow Eli Lilly researchers Bryan Molloy, Ray Fuller, Klaus Schmiegel, and other team members thought they might be on to something. They were convinced that they'd developed a drug that worked selectively (targeting only one chemical in the brain). If the new compound worked as they expected, it should have very few side effects. They were ready to test the experimental drug in people, and clinical trials began. Results were immediate and promising: their new drug effectively treated depression, and it caused few side effects. But their work was not done. They had to continue to test their new drug's safety and its efficiency at various dosages.

clinical trials: Controlled tests for a new drug done on human beings.

After nearly ten additional years of research and studies, the Eli Lilly research team was ready to release Prozac (fluoxetine hydrochloride), their new wonder drug, to the world.

Prozac

Prozac differed from other antidepressants in that it worked on one chemical in the brain, the chemical neurotransmitter called serotonin. It didn't affect several brain chemicals as other antide-pressants did—it affected only one, so it had far fewer side effects than antidepressant medications of the 1950s. With the release of Prozac a new class of antidepressants, called selective serotonin reuptake inhibitors [SSRIs], was born. Prozac was first ap-proved for sale in Belgium in 1986 and be-came available for sale in the United States in 1987. It took the country by storm.

According to Ronald R. Fieve's work, *Prozac: Questions and Answers for Patients, Family, and Physicians*, Prozac sales tripled between 1988 and 1989, to nearly $350 mil-lion in sales for that year alone. By 1990, it became the most frequently prescribed antidepressant drug in the world. Today, according to statistics put out by Prozac's manufacturer, Eli Lilly and Company, Pro-zac is approved and marketed in more than ninety countries worldwide and is used by more the ninety *million* people in the world today. Why?

neurotransmitter: Chemical in the brain that carries messages from neuron to neuron.

serotonin reuptake inhibitors [SSRIs]: Class of anti-depressants that work only on the neurotransmitter serotonin.

Prozac was the drug doctors and patients had been looking for. Finally the psychiatric world had an effective treatment for depres-sion that didn't cause the awful side effects the previous antidepres-sants had caused. Depressed people could feel better without suf-fering consequences of their drug treatment. Soon, patients were asking their doctors for Prozac, thinking that the new "happy pill" could cure them.

But the discovery and development of Prozac isn't the end of the antidepressant story. Other SSRIs have been developed (Zoloft, Luvox, Paxil, etc.) in the last decade, and as more and more people started taking this class of antidepressants, and as people took them over longer periods of time, new side effects started to emerge. These side effects (discussed in chapter six) continue to prompt

Drug treatment provides new options to those who suffer from a mood disorder.

scientists to test and refine antidepressants to make them as safe and as effective as possible.

Today, people with mood disorders have a number of drug treatment options available to them, all because of the development of these drugs over the last fifty years. The mood stabilizer lithium, the drug that Australian John Cade learned could help manic-depression in 1949, is still the drug of choice for bipolar disorders, even sixty years later. Many new MAOIs, like the drugs used to treat tuberculosis, have been developed since the 1950s, giving patients several from which to choose. The TCAs, first discovered in the late 1950s including amytriptyline and imipramine, are still common drug treatments for several psychiatric disorders. Because of the careful development of each of these classes of antidepressant medication (the MAOIs, the TCAs, and the SSRIs), patients with mood disorders have far more options in treatment than at any other time in history.

How many of the historical figures attending the fictional banquet described at the start of this chapter would have preferred to live in a world with more options? Most of these legendary figures, however, had no choice; they had to endure their disorders without any help from medication. Unlike our ancestors, we do have treatment options, but we face a challenge they didn't face: which treatment is the right one? With so many drugs available today, how can a patient or a doctor know which one to choose? Understanding how each type of drug works in the brain can help us make the right decision.

When an adolescent experiences a mood disorder, it is often dismissed as simple teenage moodiness.

Chapter Three

How Mood Disorder Drugs Work

Twelve-year-old Sam's teachers think he is showing signs of depression. At school he seems to be in another world and has difficulty focusing. He doesn't remember things as well as he used to. He doesn't care about the quality of his work the way he once did. His teachers think that Sam should see a doctor. Sam's parents are reluctant because they can't believe a boy this young could be depressed.

It's January in North Dakota, and fifteen-year-old Sandy isn't interested in being with her friends anymore. She doesn't want to spend time with her boyfriend but doesn't want to date anyone else either. She cries easily and often, and seems sad most of the time, especially since the winter months set in. She knows her blues will pass; they always do. By June, she'll be her old self again.

Quite different from his outgoing parents, fourteen-year-old Bill has always been somewhat shy and quiet. When he was younger, his family called him "the thinker" because he seemed so introspective. He says he doesn't get as upset or as sad as most of his friends or family members, but he doesn't get as excited, either.

These three teens, Sam, Sandy, and Bill, are real people. Their accounts are adapted from case studies in Dr. Miriam B. Kaufman's work, *Overcoming Teen Depression: A Guide for Parents*. Contrary to his parents' misconceptions, Sam isn't too young to have a mood

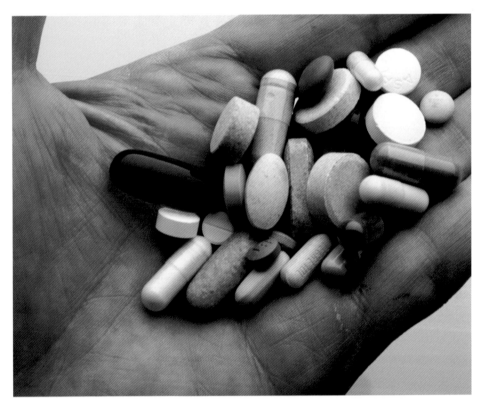

When you have a headache, you may automatically take a pill—but taking medication for a mood disorder isn't that simple. There are several questions that need to be answered first.

How a Doctor Chooses Which Drug to Prescribe

When treating a patient with a mood disorder, doctors generally weigh the answers to these five questions to determine which drug is best:

1. What is the patient's overall health condition and medical history?
2. What is the patient's diagnosis?
3. Which drugs have been proven to be most effective in treating this diagnosis?
4. How serious and long lasting are the drug's side effects?
5. Is the drug's dosing schedule something the patient can handle?

Doctors will also consider how much a drug costs (and the patient's ability to pay), how quickly the medication works, and how long the patient must be on the medication for it to work.

disorder; he is depressed, as his teachers suspect. Sam is probably experiencing a major depressive episode. Unlike Sam, Sandy suffers from a form of depression called seasonal affective disorder (SAD), which usually occurs during the winter and results from the lesser light that comes with shortened daylight hours. Our third case study, Bill, wrestles with dysthymia, or chronic mild depression—he's felt this way as long as he can remember. Though all three teenagers suffer from a different mood disorder, all three can be helped with medication. Medication isn't their only option of course (see chapter seven), but medication might help them turn their lives around.

Is medication good or bad?

Can drugs really help mood disorders?

If I take a mood disorder medication, what will it do to me?

Many teens and adults ask these kinds of questions when trying to determine how to get help for their mood disorders. They are good questions to ask.

To understand the different types of drugs used to treat depression and how they work, we have to first understand what causes depression.

What Causes Depression?

Research and case studies suggest that many different things cause depression:

- stress
- prolonged guilt
- unexpressed anger
- traumatic experiences
- extreme personal loss
- brain tumors
- disease
- brain injury

Most scientists and physicians today, however, believe that even when these other causes are present, brain biology and chemistry play a part as well. Why? Traumatic events, emotional disturbances, and physical injury can impact brain chemistry in much the same way as biological or chemical influences. In any of these cases, brain chemistry can be changed or become imbalanced enough to cause depression or other mood disorders. Depression often results from the brain producing too much or too little of certain chemicals it needs to function normally.

Neurotransmitters and Psychiatric Disorders

Scientists have identified more than twenty neurotransmitters in the brain. Here are the names of just a few of the more common neurotransmitters and some of the disorders with which they've been associated:

Neurotransmitter	Associated Psychiatric Disorders
dopamine	psychosis, schizophrenia, tic disorders, and attention-deficit hyperactivity disorder (ADHD), possibly depression
gamma-aminobutyric acid (GABA)	anxiety disorders and addictions (alcoholism and drug abuse)
glutamine	alcoholism and substance abuse
norepinephrine	depression, anxiety disorders, ADHD
serotonin	depression, obsessive-compulsive disorder (OCD)

Mood Disorders and the Drugs that Treat Them

Scientists have identified more than twenty neurotransmitters in the brain. Here are the names of just a few of the more common neurotransmitters and some of the disorders with which they've been associated:

Mood Disorder	Class of Drugs Used to Treat This Disorder	Drugs Commonly Used to Treat This Disorder: chemical name (trade name)
major depressive disorder and dysthymic disorder	antidepressants	sertraline (Zoloft) paroxetine (Paxil) fluoxetine (Prozac) fluvoxamine (Luvox) venlafaxine (Effexor) citalopram (Celexa)
bipolar disorders	mood stabilizers, atypical neuroleptics, and anticonvulsants	lithium (Lithobid, Eskalith, Cibalith) carbamazepine (Tegretol) valproate (Depakote) gabapentin (Neurontin) risperidone (Risperdal) olanzapine (Zyprexa) quetiapine (Seroquel) topiramate (Topamax)

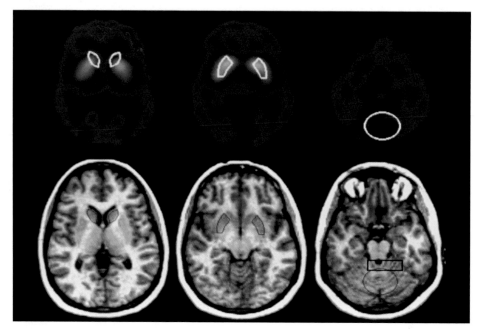

MRIs allow scientists to look inside the human skull and better understand the brain's complicated structure.

Brain Structure and Communication

Imagine that your brain is a giant communications center, the hub of all your body's communication needs. In order for your body to function, the brain must communicate with itself and with every other part of your body. According to research physicians who have studied this three-pound communications center, *billions* of messages are sent and received throughout the brain in a single day. It uses a complex network of nerve cells called neurons.

Neurons are made up of three structures: dendrites (several branch-like limbs protruding from the cell body, which receive information), the cell body (the neuron's central part, which examines information), and an axon (a single cable-like tail, which sends

Q & A

Question: If I'm depressed, shouldn't I be able to just snap out of it?

Answer: No. Not if your depression is rooted in chemical imbalances in the brain. Depression is a *disease*. No one today would say to someone with diabetes, "You don't need medication; just snap out of it." We know that diabetes is rooted in an imbalance of blood sugars. We also know that certain types of diabetes can only be controlled by taking a drug called insulin. It is no different for mood disorders. For some mood disorders, medication is the *only* means to improve symptoms. The best treatment strategies combine drug treatment with things like proper diet, exercise, and psychotherapy or counseling. Mood disorders today are treatable disorders, and most (eight out of ten patients) are successfully treated.

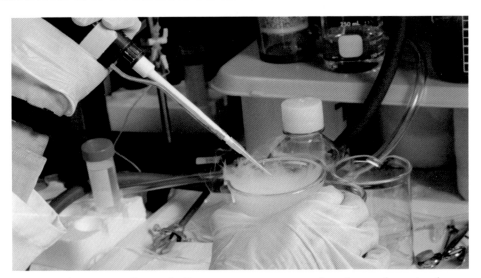

Researchers work with brain enzymes and other chemicals to determine the effects of various substances on the human mind.

information). The end of the axon contains several terminal buttons, which overlap the dendrites of other neurons. The neurons, however, don't actually touch each other; they leave a space between called the synapse.

terminal buttons: Found at the end of a neuron's axon, these attach to the dendrites of other neurons.

Communication Between Brain Cells: A Bit Like Baseball

Because neurons, the brain's nerve cells, don't actually touch each other, they must use special chemicals called neurotransmitters to send and receive messages. This sending and receiving can be a complicated process.

Imagine that you're an outfielder in a baseball game and you want to send a message to the catcher. You attach a note to the ball in your hand, wind up, swing your arm, release the ball, and throw it toward home plate. The baseball, with message attached, flies through air, across midfield, right to the catcher's glove. Though your center fielder's glove never touched the catcher's glove, you were able to get the message to him. How? You used the ball.

Neurons work together in a similar way in the brain. Using our baseball analogy, you, the center fielder, would be the sending nerve cell, called the presynaptic neuron. The message you want to send is the note attached to the baseball. The catcher would be the receiving cell, called the postsynaptic neuron. To get the message from you, the center fielder (presynaptic neuron), to the catcher (postsynaptic neuron), you have to throw the ball. In the brain, instead of using a baseball to carry the message, the presynaptic neuron (the sending nerve cell) sends its message using chemical neurotransmitters. To throw the ball, the neuron "fires," releasing the neurotransmitters (the baseball) into the synapse (the space between the nerve cells or the space between center field and home) to carry its message.

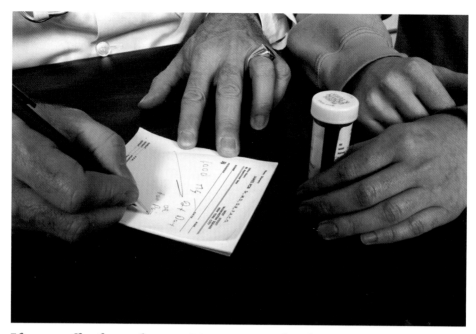

If you suffer from depression, your medical practitioner may prescribe an antidepressant.

Once released into the synapse, the neurotransmitter (the ball) looks for the postsynaptic neuron's (receiving cell's or catcher's) receptors (catcher's glove). When the presynaptic neuron's neurotransmitters bind with the postsynaptic neuron's receptors (when the ball finds its way to the glove), the message is delivered.

Once the message is delivered (once the catcher takes your note off the ball), the receiving cell (the catcher) doesn't need the neurotransmitter anymore (the ball), so it releases the neurotransmitters back into the synapse (throws the ball, without its message, back into the air between home and center field). These used neurotransmitters will remain in the synapse (the ball will stay between the home and the centerfield) until the original sending cell (the center fielder) takes them back (center fielder catches or picks up the ball). This process of taking neurotransmitters back again is called reuptake.

Now imagine that you want to send a billion messages to the catcher. You'd need quite a few baseballs to send those messages! Scientists estimate the brain uses more than a million neurons to send messages over a quadrillion synapses.

Problems in Brain Communication

Though it sounds easy, communication in the brain is a complicated process made up of several steps, any of which can run into problems:

- The presynaptic neuron doesn't fire correctly (center fielder has a poor arm).
- The brain doesn't produce enough neurotransmitters (there aren't enough balls to carry the messages).
- The postsynaptic neuron has too few receptors (catcher doesn't catch well or doesn't have a glove).
- The postsynaptic neuron's receptors get blocked (a base runner blocks the catcher's glove, keeping the catcher from catching the ball).
- Enzymes (other brain chemicals) destroy too much of the neurotransmitters remaining in the synapse (fans steal the balls before they're caught).
- Too much or too little neurotransmitter is taken back by the sending cell (the center fielder hogs the used ball or drops the ball when it's returned).

Any disruption of the communication process between neurons can result in psychological disorders.

Mood disorders result primarily from problems with neurotransmitters (how they are released, how much neurotransmitter is present, how much is taken back by the sending cell). Drugs used to treat mood disorders primarily impact how much of the neurotransmit-

What do these drugs do to the brain?

Mood Disorder Drug	Action	Used to treat which mood disorders?	Treats what other disorders?
citalopram (Celexa®)	Blocks reuptake of serotonin	depression	bulimia, panic, OCD, anxiety
fluoxetine (Prozac®)	Blocks reuptake of serotonin	depression	bulimia, panic, OCD, anxiety
fluvoxamine (Luvox®)	Blocks reuptake of serotonin	depression	bulimia, panic, OCD, anxiety
lorazepam (Ativan®)	Intensifies effects of GABA	bipolar disorders	anxiety, insomnia
paroxetine (Paxil®)	Blocks reuptake of serotonin	depression	bulimia, OCD, panic
sertraline (Zoloft®)	Blocks reuptake of serotonin	depression	anxiety
venlafaxine (Effexor®)	Blocks reuptake of norepinephrine and serotonin	depression	anxiety

ter is sent when the sending neuron fires (how many balls are thrown), how much of the neurotransmitter (if any) is received by the receiving neuron (how many balls are caught), and how much of the unused neurotransmitter is taken back by the sending cell (how many balls the center fielder takes back when the catcher is done with them). Mood disorder drugs help make sure there are enough baseballs to carry the messages between centerfield and home, and that they are caught and taken back appropriately.

norepinephrine: A type of neurotransmitter found in the brain.

dopamine: Chemical neurotransmitter in the brain.

antidepressants: A class of psychiatric drugs that treat depression.

To date, scientists have identified over one hundred kinds of neurotransmitters in the brain, with each being used in multiple parts of the brain. They have also found links between certain neurotransmitters and specific psychological conditions. Depression and bipolar disorder are both linked to the neurotransmitters serotonin, norepinephrine, and dopamine.

Drugs That Treat Depression: Antidepressants

To treat mood disorders doctors often prescribe a special class of drugs called antidepressants to influence the specific chemical balance or neuron action that is causing the disorder. Antidepressant drugs can influence brain chemistry three ways:

1. They can block the reuptake of the neurotransmitter, which causes the neurotransmitter to remain in the synapse for a longer period of time (block the center fielder from picking up returned balls).

2. They can block the receiving cell's chemical receptors, which prevents the receiving cell from getting certain messages from the sending cell (block the catcher's mitt, keeping the catcher from catching the ball).
3. They may prevent the enzymes that break down neurotransmitters from working, which causes the amount of neurotransmitter in the synapse to increase (arrest the fans before they have a chance to steal balls from midfield).

The Mayo Clinic divides antidepressant medications into five categories based on which action the medication takes and which chemicals are involved:

When a doctor writes a prescription for a psychiatric drug, her decision is based on years of scientific research.

- selective serotonin reuptake inhibitors (SSRIs), which block the reuptake of only one neurotransmitter, called serotonin, by using action one above.
- mixed reuptake inhibitors, which block the reuptake of several different kinds of neurotransmitters at once by using action one above.
- receptor blockers, which block nerve cell receptors from receiving messages by using action two above.
- reuptake inhibitors and receptor blockers, which block both the reuptake of neurotransmitters and nerve cell receptors, by using actions one and two above.
- enzyme inhibitors (MAOIs or MAO Inhibitors), which prevent certain enzymes (called monoamine oxidase) from breaking down neurotransmitters in the synapse by using action three above.

Drugs That Treat Bipolar Disorder: Mood Stabilizers

Because bipolar disorders include manic phases in addition to depression (patients experience both ups and downs), these disorders needed to be treated differently. Straight antidepressants may help the depressed phase but will do little to calm the manic phase and can even cause mania. For this reason, a different class of drugs needs to be used in bipolar patients: the mood stabilizers and anticonvulsants. The primary mood stabilizer is lithium.

Lithium

Initially used as a sedative after World War II, this element, which occurs naturally in our world, was first approved by the U.S. FDA for use in patients with bipolar disorder in 1974.

Lithium works in much the same way as the antidepressants do; it affects neurotransmitters in the brain. But how it affects the

An appropriate treatment plan depends on finding a practitioner who has experience with the particular disorder. Once medication is prescribed, there is no guarantee that the medication will work right away—and it is difficult to predict who will experience side effects. Stabilizing moods can take some time and often may require more than one medication. In many cases, a combination of medications are needed to control the symptoms of the disorder.

brain is less clear. Scientists have learned that lithium impacts the neurotransmitter called glutamate, but only in people who have abnormal levels of that particular neurotransmitter. In a person with normal levels of glutamate, lithium has no effect. The bottom line is that scientists don't really know exactly how lithium works; they only know that it does.

ion channels: Valves in the cell membrane that allow some chemicals to enter the cell, while they allow other chemicals to leave the cell.

Anticonvulsants

Another very common type of mood stabilizer used to treat bipolar disorders is the same type of drug doctors use to treat seizures. Physicians who treated convulsive patients with antiseizure medication noticed that their patients experienced less depressive symptoms and more stable moods than those who used other treatment strategies. Eventually the link was established between antiseizure medications and better mood control. This common group of drugs is called anticonvulsants.

Anticonvulsants keep people with seizure disorders from having convulsions. Because seizure activity is rooted in the electrical and chemical processes of the brain, the drugs used to treat seizures affect the brain's electrical and chemical activity. Doctors use anticonvulsants to treat people with bipolar disorder because this kind of drug acts on neuron receptors, neurotransmitters, and ion channels. They aren't sure, however, which of these actions stabilizes a person's moods.

Antidepressants?
Mood Stabilizers?
Anticonvulsants? Something Else?

If there are so many drugs available to treat mood disorders, how does a doctor know which to select? Choosing which drug to prescribe for which mood disorder is a decision a doctor will not make lightly. He considers many facts.

First, he looks at the patient's medical history. Does the patient have a health history (heart or liver disease, for example) that would make it unsafe to take certain medications? Is she currently taking other drugs for other medical conditions that wouldn't mix well with a mood disorder drug or would prevent it from working? Does she have any allergies to medication? A doctor won't prescribe a drug unless he is confident that the patient can take the drug safely.

If his patient's medical background suggests that it's safe to take a mood disorder drug, the doctor will next consider the diagnosis. Which mood disorder does the patient have, and what is its cause? These facts alone will narrow the treatment field. If sixteen-year-old Susan comes into the office clearly suffering from mood swings that are both high and low, a doctor will not prescribe a drug that treats only her lows. He'll choose drugs that stabilizes both, and not drugs that only work on one or the other. His decision is based on the diagnosis.

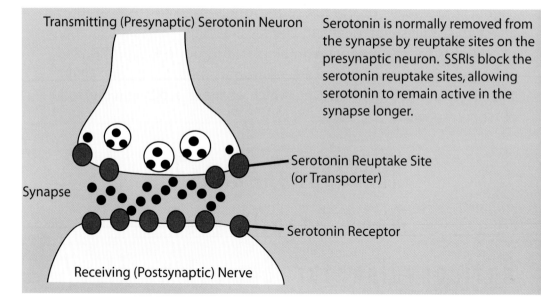

Transmitting (Presynaptic) Serotonin Neuron

Serotonin is normally removed from the synapse by reuptake sites on the presynaptic neuron. SSRIs block the serotonin reuptake sites, allowing serotonin to remain active in the synapse longer.

Serotonin Reuptake Site (or Transporter)

Synapse

Serotonin Receptor

Receiving (Postsynaptic) Nerve

Serotonin is a neurotransmitter that helps pass messages between nerve cells.

Diagnosis alone isn't enough to make a doctor pick a certain drug. Third, since not all drugs work equally well in treating various disorders, the doctor will start with drugs that have been proven to work best. In Susan's case, he'll choose from a list of drugs that are known to be most effective in treating bipolar disorders.

Once he's narrowed the options to just a few drugs, the doctor will weigh potential side effects. Which drugs have the least side effects? Which can result in serious or permanent reactions? The doctor will choose a medicine that is not only effective but that will cause the least serious and least number of side effects.

One other consideration the doctor will weigh is how often the drug needs to be taken. Some drugs for mood disorders can be taken once a day, while others have to be taken two, three, or four times daily. How likely is a teenager to remember to take her medications three times a day? When treating a teen, the doctor will choose a drug with a dosing schedule that least interferes with the patient's daily life and is most likely to be followed.

After the doctor considers each of these questions (health history, diagnosis, effectiveness of the drug, side effects, and dosing schedule), he should have a clear indication of which drug is best. That's the drug he'll prescribe.

No Miracle Cure

For some psychological disorders, psychiatric drugs seem like a miracle cure. For others, they can only control symptoms. For many, drug treatment alone doesn't work but needs to be used together with psychotherapy (talk therapy or counseling). In any case, drug treatment isn't like dispensing candy. It's a science that needs to be monitored closely by a licensed practitioner.

Mood disorder drugs influence neurotransmitters, which affect how you think, feel, and act. These drugs have the potential to greatly help lives—or greatly damage them. Only when a trained professional sets up the correct treatment protocol will mood disorder drugs do what they are intended to do with the least possibility of harm.

When an adolescent's moodiness crosses the line into a mood disorder, psychiatric medications may provide solutions.

Chapter Four

Drug Treatments

Thirteen-year-old Patrick Weaver (not his real name) stormed into the house, slammed the door, and with his backpack still slung over his shoulder, took the steps two-at-a-time to get to his room.

"Hi, honey," his mother called as he rushed by.

He answered with silence.

"I don't know, Frank," Patrick's mother confided to her husband later that evening. "Patrick's just not himself lately. He's not eating. He's lost weight. He's irritable all the time, and when he's not angry, he's sullen and withdrawn. All he does when he comes home from school is close himself off in that room. I even heard him muttering to himself in there earlier."

A medical practitioner will ask many questions before making a diagnosis of mood disorder.

"Oh, he's just thirteen. It's all that testosterone skyrocketing through his system. Look how much he's grown in the last three months—it must be two inches by now. Don't worry, Liz. It's just a teenage guy thing. It will pass."

But it didn't pass. Patrick's mood worsened over the next few weeks. When his mother heard muffled sobs behind his bedroom door one afternoon, she paused to listen to his mumblings.

"I just don't want to live anymore," he choked. "All they do is laugh at me. God, why are you doing this? Just let me die."

His mother quietly opened his door, and there on the bed was Patrick, doubled over like he was in pain, clutching his pillow to his chest.

Patrick was depressed; there was no doubt about it. And he needed more help than his parents could give. Patrick's mother called a family friend who happened to be a psychologist who specialized in treating adolescents.

Q & A

Question: What can I expect to happen at an appointment with a psychiatrist or other mental health professional?

Answer: During your first visit to a medical professional you can expect to:

- Be treated with professionalism, respect, and appropriate concern.
- Be allowed to have a family member with you at the appointment.
- Spend at least an hour at the appointment.
- Answer detailed questions about your medical history.
- Complete a survey (called a "Patient Questionnaire") about your recent symptoms.
- Meet with the doctor.
- Discuss your symptoms with the doctor.
- Have a physical exam (if this was not previously done).
- Be given the opportunity to ask questions.
- Have your questions answered.
- Possibly be referred for additional medical tests.
- Possibly be referred for counseling or psychotherapy.
- Possibly be put on psychiatric medication.
- Be scheduled for follow-up visits.
- Be free (sometimes encouraged) to get a second opinion.

"I could see him, if you like, Liz," their psychologist friend offered. "But I think Patrick needs to see a medical doctor for a complete physical evaluation. First, you need to rule out any other illnesses that might be causing Patrick's symptoms."

I wonder what we'll find out, Patrick's mother wondered as she made the appointment. *What kinds of test will they do?* What could she and Patrick expect when they met with the family doctor?

When you suspect that you or a loved one may have a mood disorder, do what Patrick's mother did: make an appointment for a complete physical with your regular physician. The doctor may talk with you about how you're feeling; she may ask questions about symptoms; she may discuss your eating habits, sleep patterns, and exercise; she will probably do a routine neurological exam (like testing your reflexes by tapping your knee); she may test your blood for viruses or other infections that might cause fatigue, irritability, or other

Blood tests may help medical practitioners understand what's causing a person's symptoms.

Questions to Ask If Your Doctor Prescribes Medication

The American Academy of Child and Adolescent Psychiatry recommends asking the doctor who prescribes your medication several questions. What follows is adapted from their list.

1. What is the medication's name? What are its other names?
2. Has this medication helped other people my age? How?
3. What will the medication do for me? How long will it take to work?
4. What side effects can I expect? How long will they last? Will they go away?
5. What other rare and dangerous side effects are possible?
6. Can I become addicted to this medication? Can it be abused?
7. What will be my dosage to start? What is the recommended dosage?
8. Will I have to take special tests to monitor this drug in my system (blood tests, heart tests, liver tests, etc.)?
9. What foods or medicines should I avoid while taking this drug?
10. Are there any activities I can't do while I'm on this drug?
11. How long will I have to be on this medication?
12. How do I go off this medication safely?
13. What do I do if I have problems with this drug?
14. Do I have to inform my school officials or school nurse that I'm taking this drug?
15. Who else needs to know that I'm on this drug?

symptoms that are typical of mood disorders. Or she may order additional lab tests based on what she learns from talking with you.

This is what Patrick's doctor did, and much to the family's relief, apart from Patrick's recent weight loss, everything was normal. But Patrick wasn't "fine." Now what were they supposed to do?

"Take him to see a reputable psychiatrist in your area," the Weavers' psychologist friend suggested when Patrick's mother called him again. "I can give you a few names, but look for a psychiatrist who specializes in treating adolescents. Children and teens often have different symptoms than adults, even for the same disorders. And psychiatric drugs that work in adults may not work in kids. You need to see someone who knows how to treat teenagers Patrick's age."

Once your family doctor rules out other medical causes, if your symptoms continue, it's time to see a psychiatrist—especially if your symptoms keep you from feeling, thinking, or acting normally. For youth and teens it's vital that the psychiatrist have experience working with adolescents for the reasons the Weavers' psychologist friend suggested. As a specialist in adolescent psychology, the family friend knew that treatment plans for adults don't always work in teens. Even the drugs used vary.

If he was well-trained in counseling adolescents, why didn't the Weaver's friend opt to treat Patrick? Probably because he was a psychologist, not a psychiatrist. What's the difference? It's an important distinction.

Only medical doctors can write prescriptions for psychiatric drugs. Psychiatrists are medical doctors who specialize in disorders of the mind, just like neurologists are medical doctors who specialize in treating problems with the nervous system, or oncologists are medical doctors who specialize in treating cancer. Advanced practice nurses can also have training in psychiatry; they can diagnose, do therapy, and write prescriptions. Psychologists, however, have special training and education in counseling, but they are not medical doctors. Psychologists cannot write prescriptions for medication; psychiatrists and advanced practice nurses can.

What do these drugs do to the brain?

Name of Drug	Average Adolescent Daily Dose	How long does it take to work?	How long does it take my body to get rid of half of the drug? (half-life)
amitriptyline (Elavil®)	Total: 50–300 mg. over 4 doses	Side effects: within a few doses Improvements: 2-4 weeks	20-46 hours
carbamazepine (Tegretol®)	Total: 200–1000 mg. over 2 doses	Side effects: 1–2 days Improvement in mania: 1–2 weeks	Initially: 25–64 hours, after steady use: 12-17 hours
fluoxetine (Prozac®)	Total: 5–40 mg. over 1–2 doses	Side effects: 1–2 days Improvements: 2-4 weeks	1-3 days
lithium carbonate (Lithonate®)	Total: 900–1800 mg. over 2–3 doses	Improvement in mania: 1–3 weeks	18–24 hours
sertraline (Zoloft®)	Total: 25–200 mg. over 1–2 doses	Side effects: 1–2 days Improvement: 2-4 weeks	25 hours
venlafaxine (Effexor®)	Total: 75–150 mg. over 2-3 doses	Side effects: 1–2 days Improvement: 2-4 weeks	3-7 hours

The Weavers' friend may have decided not to treat Patrick because he suspected that Patrick's symptoms might require drug treatment, something he could not provide. He knew that a psychiatrist could.

At their friend's recommendation, Mrs. Weaver called a psychiatrist who specialized in treating adolescents, Dr. Reed, and set up an appointment for the following week.

"Patrick, we need you to fill out the paper that's attached to this clipboard," Dr. Reed's receptionist instructed as the Weavers checked in for Patrick's appointment.

"Mom, I don't want to do this," Patrick whined. "You do it for me."

"No, Patrick. This appointment is for you," his mother encouraged. "The doctor needs to know whether or not you've ever felt or thought about the things on this list, not whether or not I have. For

A pharmacist carefully counts the medication when filling a prescription.

Dr. Reed to help you, he needs you to tell him as much as you can about how you've been feeling. Completing this form will help you do that."

During a first visit with a mental health professional, patients like Patrick are often requested to complete a questionnaire that asks about certain symptoms. According to the Mayo Clinic Foundation's *Mayo Clinic on Depression*, questionnaires or surveys of this kind may ask questions like these:

- Over the past month, have you experienced a loss of interest in activities you used to enjoy?
- Do you feel hopeless?
- Do you have trouble falling asleep at night?
- Do you feel tired most of the time?
- Have you ever wished you were dead? When? How often?
- Have you ever thought about hurting yourself in some way?
- Do you have trouble concentrating or making decisions?
- Has your appetite changed?
- Do you feel fidgety and restless?

The questions on the survey correlate exactly to symptoms of various disorders listed in the *Diagnostic and Statistical Manual*, fourth edition, text revision (DSM-IV-TR). When you answer the questions honestly, the survey can provide important information to the doctor to help her make the proper diagnosis.

Once you complete the questionnaire, the psychiatrist may ask questions about some of your answers, or she may ask questions about your overall health. This initial discussion may take an hour or two, but unless you have a very complicated mood disorder, your psychiatrist may be able to identify which mood disorder you have just from the facts and observations she makes during this initial visit.

That's exactly what happened for Patrick.

After Dr. Reed interviewed Patrick and his mother, and after he went over Patrick's questionnaire, the psychiatrist was certain that

A Common Treatment Plan
for Mood Disorders

Step One: Rule out underlying medical issues that may be causing the disorder.

Step Two: Carefully evaluate the patient for suicide potential. If necessary, hospitalize.

Step Three: Begin the appropriate psychiatric drug. For major depressive disorder: SSRIs (Prozac, Paxil, Zoloft, Effexor, etc.). For bipolar disorder: lithium or Depakote.

Step Four: Consider psychotherapy in addition to Step Three.

Step Five: Where necessary, gradually increase amount of medication until the patient reaches full dose (or therapeutic level). Always use the lowest effective dose.

Step Six: In bipolar disorders, watch the patient for signs of mania.

Step Seven: In depressive disorders, wait four to six weeks for improvement.

Step Eight: In bipolar disorder, stop the antidepressant when the depression resolves but keep the patient on lithium or Depakote to prevent further manic episodes.

Step Nine: After four to six weeks, consider drug's effectiveness. If not working, change.

Adapted from Dr. Jack Gorman's *The Essential Guide to Psychiatric Drugs.*

Patrick was suffering from depression. Medication combined with psychotherapy and exercise was the treatment plan.

"Patrick, I think you're depressed. Your symptoms are consistent with what we call major depressive disorder. That's the bad news. The good news is that many kids, more than you think, have this condition, and it is fully treatable."

"What do you mean treatable? What do I have to do?"

"Well, I'd like you to start getting some regular exercise—maybe you can rejoin your soccer team. And I'd like to meet with you once a week for a while just to talk about some of the things you mentioned on your survey. But I'd also like to start you out on a drug we often use to treat depression in teenagers. It's called Zoloft. When it comes to your drug treatment, all you have to do is to remember to take the drug once a day."

"Will the pill make me feel sick?"

"It might upset your stomach or bother your intestines, but only for a short time after you take the pill, and only for a week or so. As your body gets used to the drug, you may notice some other minor side effects, too."

"Like what?"

"Your mouth might feel dry and you might not feel very hungry. You might experience headaches or dizziness, and you might have difficulty going to sleep at night. But none of these should last. Once your body adjusts, those symptoms should go away . . . usually in one to two weeks." Dr. Reed paused, giving Patrick time to think about what he'd just said and to come up with any other questions.

Patrick dug the toe of his shoe into the carpet. "How much do I have to take?"

"We always begin with the lowest dose available to make sure you can tolerate the medication. I think we'll start you off on twenty-five milligrams. Then in a week, if all goes well, we'll increase to fifty, but let's see how you respond to twenty-five first."

"Is that a lot?"

"No. It's what we start most kids on."

"How do I take it?

"It comes as a small, light green capsule-shaped tablet. You can swallow pills, right?"

Patrick glanced over at his mom, then nodded.

"Then take one caplet with a big glass of water every morning."

"How long will it take to help me . . . I mean . . . when will I start to feel better?"

"Don't expect to feel better tomorrow. It might take four to six weeks for you to notice much improvement. I'd like to see you in two weeks here at the office to talk about how you're feeling and to see how you're doing with the drug."

Dr. Reed paused. "You're doing a great job here, Patrick. You're asking about a lot of really important things. Do you have any other questions before we wrap up?"

"Yeah. How long do I have to do this . . . take medication, I mean."

"We'll try it for six months. By then your depression may be gone, and we can start to take you off the medication. But you can't just quit taking it all at once. We need to taper you off slowly."

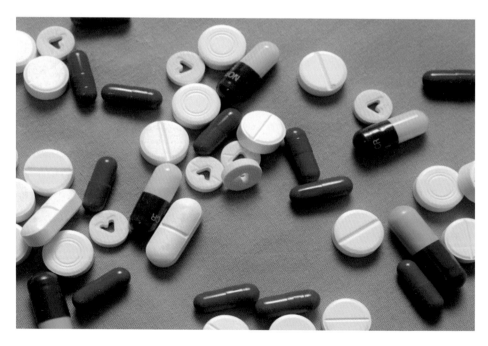

Medication comes in many shapes and sizes.

Dr. Reed looked at Patrick's mother, then at Patrick. "I'm optimistic that we can help Patrick, but we'll know more in a couple of weeks. If you have any side effects from the medication, feel free to give me a call. Don't forget, Patrick, that I want to see you back here in two weeks when we can talk some more. Your mom can make an appointment for you with the receptionist on the way out."

Patrick and his mother were glad they had gone to a psychiatrist who could give him the help he needed. But when Patrick's doctor suggested drug treatment, Patrick had questions. He asked the right ones: How much of the drug would I have to take? How will I take it? How long would it take to take effect? What should I expect when I take the drug? These questions should be answered before starting on any drug treatment regimen.

regimen: A regular, systematic plan.

Pill Forms,
Administration, and Duration

The answers to Patrick's questions will not be the same for every drug or every patient. Treatment regimens are tailored to suit the patient's needs. Each patient is different, and the drugs used are different as well. Each drug has its own forms, concentrations, and methods of being taken. There is no "one size fits all."

The best source of answers to questions about any medication is, of course, your doctor. But many questions can be answered by reading the pharmacist's fact sheet (information about a drug that pharmacists supply when they fill your prescription), by reading the package insert (a paper supplied in the drug package by the manufacturer listing facts about the drug), or by looking the drug up in a reference book called the *Physician's Desk Reference* (PDR; for more information about package inserts and the PDR, see chapter six). But some generalizations can be made.

Most antidepressants, mood stabilizers, and anticonvulsants come in swallowable capsule or tablet form—they aren't usually shots or chewable tablets. Some, like Zoloft, come in a liquid form for the patient to drink. But form isn't the only thing that varies between medications. Dose frequency can be different from drug to drug, too.

Some mood disorder medications are designed to be taken several times daily; others can be taken once a day or once a week. Some act immediately (meaning that they are released into your body's system all at once and start to work right away) while others are sustained-release (meaning that they are released gradually into your body over time and start to work after some delay). Immediate-acting medications must be taken multiple times a day with less time between doses because they absorb quickly into the body and then readily dissipate. Medications that only have to be taken once a day or once a week (the sustained-release kind) metabolize more slowly, so they last longer in the body.

The amount of medication in each drug form can also vary. Manufacturers often supply several different forms and concentrations of the same drug. Zoloft, the drug Dr. Reed prescribed for Patrick, comes in twenty-five-, fifty-, and one-hundred-milligram tablets that are scored so they can be cut in half. This makes it easy to adjust dosages. If a doctor prescribes fifty milligrams of Zoloft daily, then needs to increase the dose to seventy-five, the patient can take three twenty-five-milligram tablets, or one fifty-milligram tablet and cut another fifty-milligram tablet in half. As long as he's getting his accurate dosage amount, it doesn't really matter which pill form he takes.

dissipate: To break up, disappear.

metabolize: To biochemically change the characteristics of a food substance.

Some pill forms, however, tend to work better for patients than others. For example, some patients may not have the kind of schedule that would allow them to take medication four times a day. A sustained-release version of the same drug, which only has to be taken once a day, would be a better choice for them. Some patients prefer sustained-release versions to immediate-acting ones because the effects of the medication are less intense and more balanced over time. Others, because of difficulty swallowing larger pills, may prefer smaller immediate-acting forms.

When he prescribed Zoloft, Dr. Reed prescribed a medication that was well suited to Patrick's dosing needs. Since he only had to take his medication once a day, it was easy for him to remember to take it—he just took it every morning before breakfast. Because Patrick was using the twenty-five-milligram tablets, his doctor could easily adjust his dose. When he moved from twenty-five milligrams to fifty, he could just take two tablets instead of one.

"So what do you think?" Liz asked her son on the way home in the car.

Patrick shrugged.

"How do you feel about taking medication?" she prodded.

Patrick sighed. "Do the kids at school have to know?"

"Of course not," his mother assured him. "We will have to tell the school nurse so she has it in her files, but that's all. No one else has to know."

"What if it doesn't work?"

"There are lots of other treatment options out there. This is only one. But let's try what Dr. Reed tells us, and then we can wait and see. The most important thing is that we know what you're dealing with now and you're getting the help you need. It's a great start. Now all we have to do is watch out for those side effects."

A mood disorder may change a person's entire outlook on life.

Chapter Five

Real People with Mood Disorders

What would you do if one day you woke up and discovered that you weren't yourself anymore? Your personality had changed, and you just weren't the happy-go-lucky, positive person you'd always been? What if everything you knew and loved became meaningless to you? What if everything you looked forward to and dreamed about seemed like impossibilities that could never be reached? What if you just didn't want to live anymore?

Leesha

Fourteen-year-old Leesha, a once happy, carefree freshman who excelled in school, couldn't understand what was happening to her.

She no longer enjoyed her classes. She had little energy or enthusiasm for anything, even for pep club, student council, and cheerleading—all of which had meant the world to her before. Once a conscientious student, she didn't care that her research paper was late, that she'd missed her appointment with her guidance counselor, or that her French teacher was asking about recently missed homework assignments. She just didn't care, period. *What's wrong with me?* Leesha wondered.

Thinking that maybe it was just a phase, Leesha plugged on, not telling anyone about the dark thoughts that swirled through her head. *Just quit*, the thoughts told her. *Don't even bother going to school. No one will care. You can't do anything right anymore, so why try? Just walk away, and don't look back.*

On some days, this one-time honor roll student listened to the voices and skipped school. Other times she went to class, but she barely listened to what the teacher said. She was too deep in her own dark thoughts.

Leesha's grades plummeted. Her cheerleading coach kicked her off the squad for missing too many practices. Her friends started to drift away, tired of always trying to cheer up their melancholy friend. To avoid her mother's nagging, Leesha started not coming home from school and staying out until late in the evening. She just wanted to be left alone.

But Leesha's mom wouldn't leave her alone. She worried about Leesha's changing behavior and expressed her growing fears to a friend of hers who had a doctorate in family counseling. He invited Leesha to meet with him and her parents for counseling, but Leesha and her father turned him down. *I don't need help from some stupid counselor,* the teen thought. *He won't be able to help anyway.* Not going for counseling ensured that Leesha wouldn't get help, and without help, her symptoms grew worse. Now the dark thoughts weren't just about skipping school; they told her to skip life.

Leesha's mom continued meeting with the counselor, even though no one else in the family would go. Convinced that Lee-

Q & A

Question: When various school shootings have been in the news, it seems that some reporter always suggests that psychiatric drugs make people violent. I've heard stories saying that psychiatric drugs cause people to do violent things. Is it true?

Answer: Dr. Ronald R. Fieve, in his book, *Prozac*, reminds the reader that mood disorder drugs won't always work the way they are intended. Some mood disorder drugs can actually have the opposite effect. By the same token, sometimes they don't work at all. This is just the nature of medications, and it doesn't happen any more frequently in mood disorder drugs than it does in other drugs. In very rare instances, some researchers have linked the taking of mood disorder drugs with unexpected changes in behavior, including agitation, outbursts of anger, psychotic episodes, and irrational acts. There is not sufficient evidence, however, to say that these drugs *cause* people to do violence. Other factors are far more likely to cause or influence that kind of behavior. Drugs may lower the patients' self-restraint or inhibition, but they don't *make* a person take a specific action.

sha was clinically depressed, he urged Leesha's mother to take her daughter to a psychiatrist.

Leesha's mother and the counselor weren't the only ones who were concerned. Leesha herself was becoming desperate and more fearful of her spiraling, out-of-control thoughts and feelings. The ninth-grader was tired of always being tired. She wanted help. Finally, she told her mother she was ready to see the psychiatrist.

Leesha's father wouldn't be swayed, though. He thought that psychiatrists were for "crazy people." "No daughter of mine is going to see some shrink!" he insisted. Leesha feared her father more than she feared her illness, so she backed down and didn't go. Things got worse.

Leesha felt like she was in a dark tunnel—an endless, lifeless chasm—with no way out. The tension between her parents mounted. Now her folks fought all the time: Leesha's mom tried to convince her father that their daughter needed help; Leesha's father denied that anything was wrong. Because of the constant conflict at home, Leesha's father started drinking more, and their fights escalated. Her father stayed out late and came home drunk.

I hate this! I can't stand it anymore! I just want out! Why can't everyone just leave me alone!!! Leesha couldn't take it. She'd had enough. On the day when Leesha finally decided she could endure it no more, her parents received a phone call from the local hospital. Leesha had attempted suicide.

Doctors advised Leesha's parents to admit her to a short-stay psychiatric unit. Once she was admitted, psychiatrists diagnosed the struggling teen as having major depressive disorder. They started her on a drug treatment regimen. But drugs wouldn't be enough to help Leesha. As part of her treatment, she and her family were required to participate in group, family, and individual counseling. In group therapy sessions, her parents met and interacted with families with similar problems. Leesha's father was relieved to learn that other families had gone through the same thing; they were not alone.

The help and support Leesha's parents received from group therapy and the skills they learned in family and individual counseling enabled them to give Leesha the support and understanding she needed to get through her treatment and recovery. After two weeks in the psychiatric ward and being on the right antidepressant, Leesha began to feel her old self emerging. She was slowly climbing out of the pit and into the daylight again.

When she went home, Leesha's energy, enthusiasm, and motivation returned. She finished out her freshman year as the A-student

Depression should be taken seriously, as it can cause a person to take desperate action. Friends and family need to offer help and support, while medication may offer relief from the sadness.

Suicide Facts

- According to the American Association of Suicidology, suicide is the tenth leading cause of death for people of all ages. For those aged fifteen to twenty-four, suicide is the third leading cause of death.
- Statistics Canada reported in 2009 that suicide is the leading cause of death for Canadians between the ages of fifteen and thirty-four.
- In a recent report on depression, the U.S. Surgeon General noted that people with bipolar disorder were twenty-five times more likely to commit suicide as the general population.
- Adolescents with depressive disorders are five times more likely to attempt suicide as their non-depressed peers.
- Most people who commit suicide talk about it first. If someone you know talks about suicide or mentions suicidal thoughts or attempts, take their comments seriously! Report their comments to a responsible adult immediately.

she'd previously been. With the combined help of medication, therapy, and family support, Leesha was depressed no more.

This case study, adapted from an account written by Marilyn Sargent of the National Institute for Mental Health, illustrates a few key points about treating mood disorders in adolescents:

- First, depression in teens is not a "phase" adolescents will grow out of. If Leesha and her father had been more willing to get help earlier in her decline, perhaps they would have been spared her suicide attempt.

- Second, dark thoughts of death and suicide should always be taken seriously. The National Mental Heath Association notes that nearly all people who attempt suicide speak about it (and think about it) first.

- Third, getting help for a mood disorder requires more than just popping a pill. Learning how to communicate with family members, how to reduce stress, how to cope with and manage feelings—these are all parts of the recovery process. Counseling and therapy, in addition to medication, are often necessary to help a person with a mood disorder get well.

- Fourth, if you are depressed or struggling with another kind of mood disorder, you can't beat it on your own. The good news is that help is available today that can effectively treat your symptoms and get you back on the road of normal life. You just need to be willing to ask for and receive the help you need.

Leesha's experience with clinical depression, though difficult to live through, resulted in help for her and her family. Unfortunately, not every case study has a happy ending.

Stephen Leith

What would you do if your high school chemistry teacher, once a calm, pleasant, likable guy, literally ran into the classroom one morning and started racing around your lab stations? What if, instead of discussing molecular structure and chemical formulas, he started talking about private, personal things? What if, instead of treating students with respect and cautious concern, he started making lewd remarks and touching your classmates inappropriately? If you were anything like the students in Mr. Leith's chemistry class, you'd grow increasingly more uncomfortable and begin to fear what used to be your favorite teacher.

High school chemistry teacher Stephen Leith, who taught in central Michigan's Chelsea School District in the early 1990s, had once

A person with a mood disorder is not necessarily always depressed—sometimes he may be "manic." During these emotional highs, he may lose his normal sense of inhibition.

been a popular, effective chemistry teacher. Students liked him, he taught well, and he'd earned a solid reputation with other educators. Then doctors diagnosed his wife with cancer.

As he watched his wife's health decline, Mr. Leith grew increasingly more despondent. Helpless to ease her suffering, he fell into despair. In January 1992, suspecting he was depressed, the chemistry teacher sought psychiatric help. The psychiatrist confirmed Mr. Leith's suspicions; Mr. Leith was depressed, and the doctor immediately put him on the antidepressant Prozac. Two weeks later, however, the teacher's bizarre behavior began.

In his letter to FDA Commissioner Jane Henney, M.D., dated March 22, 2000, Mr. Leith describes the change:

After about two weeks it [the Prozac] kicked in, and I was full of energy. I felt as though I could accomplish anything I put my mind to and began a major project.

People in the school where I taught knew something had happened to me: I ran everywhere, even in the school! The kids joked that I was "hitting the acid cabinet" in the back of my chemistry room, and the Superintendent, thinking I was on street drugs, called me in his office, and demanded to know what was going on.

I lost all discretion regarding what I said, even speaking to strangers about personal things. I became obnoxious and the students started fearing me, especially when I began touching some of them. I now lacked control.

After about six weeks, I sprained my ankle and the good feeling turned bad. My sleep became increasingly more fitful and the depression returned. The psychiatrist suggested taking me off Prozac, but I begged him to leave me on it, fearing the depression would be much worse without it."

Mr. Leith's letter goes on to describe his steady decline in mental health. It describes his chronic headaches and agitation. It re-

chronic: A condition characterized by long duration or frequent recurrence.

When Is It Time to Get Help?

If you recognize these symptoms in yourself or a loved one seek help:

- Frequent sadness, tearfulness, crying, helplessness
- Bouts of hostility or rage
- Low energy or lack of interest in activities
- Overreaction to criticism, rejection, or failure
- Low self-esteem or destructive self-criticism
- Unusual irritability or anger
- Desire to withdraw or be alone, or a pervading sense of isolation
- Frequent stomachaches or headaches
- Poor concentration or inability to make decisions
- Changes in school performance (skipping school, slipping grades)
- Sleep trouble (either not being able to sleep or sleeping too much)
- Eating trouble (not eating or eating too much)
- Cutting, or other ways of physically hurting oneself
- Increased use of drugs or alcohol
- Thoughts or discussions of suicide

counts that he became paranoid, thinking that people, especially superiors at his school, "were out to get [him]." He lost all sense of self-control and inhibition. He racked up massive debt, which he could not pay off. He developed a deep-rooted anger and explosive temper unlike anything he'd experienced before going on Prozac. And all the while, his wife's health worsened; she was going to die.

In addition to his psychological and emotional problems, the teacher's mental abilities got worse. His thinking grew increasingly unclear. He felt "confused much of the time" and it was difficult to teach. Mr. Leith recounts that his "brain felt like it was sloshing in [his] skull."

What happens next is a matter of public record. After nearly two years of disintegrating mental health, Mr. Leith snapped.

On December 16, 1993, Stephen Leith was scheduled to meet with Chelsea School's Superintendent Joseph Piasecki to discuss Mr. Leith's inappropriate conduct while in school. The chemistry teacher's disturbing behavior had been disciplined before, but his strange, disruptive actions continued, so a grievance hearing was called. Mr. Leith met with Piasecki as planned, but no one anticipated what happened next.

paranoid: Suffering from a condition characterized by the development of a complicated and elaborate thinking pattern based on a misinterpretation of an actual event. Sometimes includes overly suspicious behavior.

inhibition: An unconscious defense mechanism against inappropriate behaviors.

According to the *Detroit News* and the *Michigan Education Report*, after his hearing with Piasecki, Mr. Leith left Piasecki's office at the high school, went to his car, got a nine-millimeter pistol, returned to the Superintendent's office, shot Piasecki, wounded two others, then went back to his classroom. Superintendent Piasecki died of gunshot wounds. Mr. Leith's letter to the FDA describes what happened next:

> Only minutes later I was going about my normal routine in the classroom, wondering if the shooting had really transpired; it did not seem real. Of course, I was arrested and whisked away. When the lawyer arrived at the jail, I asked him if anyone got hurt!

Can you imagine your chemistry teacher shooting someone in the office, returning to class like nothing happened, then wondering if anyone had been hurt? Teens in Michigan didn't have to imagine—this was real.

Mr. Leith was tried and found guilty of murder, and is serving a life sentence in the Carson Correctional Facility in Carson City, Michigan. Two years after his arrest, his wife died of the cancer he knew would eventually kill her. With his wife dead, his career over, his reputation ruined, and a future filled only with life behind bars, why would Mr. Leith bother writing to the FDA?

Mr. Leith was pleading with the FDA to recognize that the antidepressant Prozac was a dangerous drug; he wanted them to pull it off the market. He concludes his letter with these sentences:

> So here I am, a trained educator, being punished for something I would not have done if I had not been on Prozac . . . many lives besides my own have been negatively impacted due to what Prozac did to me. This drug is dangerous. . . . Declare this drug unsafe and take it off the market.

Stephen Leith's experience with depression and its treatment is not a success story. There is no happy ending here. What should have been a treatable depression, a single mood disorder, spiraled into cycling manic and depressed phases and ultimately, paranoia, too. The result? The superintendent of his school district is dead. Mr. Leith is in prison and will be for the rest of his natural life. His wife died alone, while her husband sat in jail. The damage done by Mr. Leith cannot be undone. But his account, like Leesha's, can teach us a few things:

First, drugs used to treat mood disorders are still drugs, and like any other drug, they can have dangerous side effects. Though the FDA requires that drug manufacturers prove that a drug is "safe" for most people and that it works as it's supposed to work before they can sell it to the public, the FDA cannot guarantee that the drug will work or be safe for all people. Taking medication, any medication, comes with risks. Though it is unclear how much of Mr. Leith's symptoms resulted from his taking Prozac and how much could be attributed to an additional, existing, undiagnosed psychiatric disorder (perhaps bipolar disorder or schizophrenia), his story should still caution us about the use of medications.

Second, if you've been diagnosed with a mood disorder and your doctor prescribes medication, watch for possible side effects and report them to your doctor immediately, no matter how small they seem. Everything Mr. Leith experienced—from his energy spurts, headaches, and agitation to his uncontrolled anger and paranoia—had been documented as possible, though unlikely, side effects of Prozac.

Third, if you experience unwanted reactions to a drug, be willing to try a different drug treatment or alternate therapy. Mr. Leith could have been weaned from Prozac and given a different medication, or he could have sought counseling, but he refused to do so, even after his psychiatrist recommended that he go off the drug.

Though Mr. Leith's mental state changed dramatically after taking Prozac, and though the drug may have caused many of his symptoms, experts disagree as to whether or not Prozac is to blame for his murderous rampage. What is clear is that Mr. Leith's treatment for depression, and his unwillingness to change treatment when he suffered side effects, contributed to his mental breakdown. That leads us to a very important question: Does treating mood disorders with drugs pose any real, substantiated danger for the patient? What are the risks involved? Is treatment worth the risk?

Suicide is a risk factor for many mood disorders.

Chapter Six

Risks and Side Effects

Fifteen-year-old Sarah sought psychiatric help for the anxiety and depression she experienced as a result of her parents' bitter divorce. Her doctor prescribed the antidepressant Paxil, an SSRI. For the next year, though, Sarah lost all interest in the opposite sex.

Doctors put Florida college student Cora on Prozac, another SSRI, to overcome mild depression, but she found only partial help in her small starting dose. Gradually, over the next three months, Cora's physician increased her dosage to 80 milligrams. Ten days after reaching the full 80-milligram dosage, Cora ended up in the emergency room with her jaw frozen shut and muscles spasms in her tongue and neck.

Two weeks after starting a daily 20-milligram regimen of an antidepressant doctors prescribed for his psychiatric disorder, a fifteen-

Serious Adverse Reactions to Treat as an Emergency

If you experience any of the following symptoms after taking a mood disorder medication, call your doctor immediately:

- shortness of breath
- chest discomfort
- severe agitation
- hallucinations
- disorientation or mental confusion
- fainting or loss of consciousness
- seizure, tics, or other neurological events
- suicidal thoughts or urges

year-old youth with obsessive-compulsive disorder (OCD), but with no known history of depression, hanged himself in a suicide attempt. He died.

These three scenarios, all of which are actual case studies taken from Dr. Joseph Glenmullen's book *Prozac Backlash*, illustrate the downside of using drugs to treat psychiatric disorders. All drugs, no matter how well tested, come with risks, and not all risks are known before the patient starts taking medication.

As ominous as this sounds, it's important to remember that most side effects (called adverse reactions) associated with FDA-approved drugs are *minor* if patients use the drugs according to their doctors' instructions and for the purpose for which they were designed. When a patient does not use a drug as the doctor directs (taking too much, for example, or mixing the drug with alcohol) or when the patient uses the drug for purposes other than for what it was intended (using prescribed drugs to get high, mixing that drug with

Medications do not work for everyone and cannot save every patient's life. Sometimes the wrong prescription can be deadly—but more people have probably committed suicide because they did not receive therapy or medication treatment. In many cases, the patient's quality of life improves from the medication. People who were once suicidal have gone on to lead fulfilling lives free from depression.

other drugs, passing the drugs around to their friends), the consequences can be deadly. For their own safety and the safety of those around them, people who take psychiatric drugs should follow their doctors' directions exactly.

Even when taken exactly as prescribed, however, psychiatric drugs can still sometimes cause unwanted reactions.

Common Adverse Reactions to Psychiatric Drugs

When sixteen-year-old Diane told her family physician that she couldn't remember the last time she felt happy, he immediately suspected dysthymia (chronic depression). The attentive doctor had already noticed that Diane seemed quiet and withdrawn. As they talked further, he discovered that Diane had been feeling this way for nearly two years, but she couldn't explain why she felt the way she did. All she knew was that she felt sad and cynical "all the time." She also complained of having no energy.

When a complete physical examination ruled out any other medical cause for Diane's fatigue and low energy levels, her family physician recommended that the teen talk to her parents about getting some counseling. In the meantime, with her mother's consent, he put Diane on 20 milligrams of Prozac.

In just two weeks, Diane began to improve. Her energy levels increased, she wasn't so melancholic, and school didn't seem so overwhelming anymore. Diane could think more clearly and seemed more upbeat. She even started laughing again—something her family and friends hadn't seen in a long, long time.

But Diane noticed some new symptoms: after taking Prozac for three or four days, she felt nauseated. She also had frequent headaches—not sharp pain, just the dull, throbbing kind. And, though her energy levels were rising, she sometimes felt sleepy.

Diane was experiencing side effects common to Prozac and other antidepressants: stomach or intestinal upset, headaches, drowsiness, and fatigue. Other mild adverse reactions to these drugs include dry mouth, dizziness, rash, sweating, tremors, or feeling agitated, jittery, or nervous.

Diane's doctor knew that these symptoms were side effects of Prozac, and he felt confident they would pass in time. Sure enough,

When a person is experiencing a mood disorder, medications should be carefully monitored because of the risk of suicide.

Q & A

Question: How can a drug be "safe" when the PDR (or package insert) lists so many scary adverse reactions?

Answer: The FDA requires that the manufacturer list every side effect reported or observed in any individual who has taken the drug, even if it only occurs once in five thousand cases. An individual patient is most likely never going to experience these extreme reactions. These reactions are rare. Also, when the FDA approves a drug as safe, it doesn't mean that the drug will never do harm. Cancer-fighting drugs, for example, while killing cancer cells, also make a person sick in the process. The benefit of taking the drug (curing cancer) makes it worth the risk or consequences (dealing with nausea and vomiting). "Safe" in FDA terminology means that a drug's benefit outweighs its risk and that the drug will work well without putting most patients' lives or health in jeopardy.

as with most mild adverse events, Diane's symptoms disappeared as her body got used to Prozac's effect on her system.

Package Inserts and the PDR

The primary source of information about a drug's possible side effects is a document found inside every medication package sold in the United States. That document, a single sheet of fine-print covered paper stuffed inside the medicine's external packaging, is called the package insert. You've seen them every time you've pulled an aspirin bottle or cold remedy out of its box and a tightly folded piece of paper covered with technical-looking writing falls out. That folded piece of paper is the package insert.

When a drug is sold in the United States, the FDA requires the manufacturer to provide a complete written report on the drug: what the drug is made of; how the drug is to be used; how much of the drug to prescribe, what foods or other drugs to avoid while taking this drug, possible side effects or dangers associated with the drug, what form the drug comes in (tablet? liquid? capsule?), for whom the drug should be prescribed, and so on. The package insert, which is written by the drug manufacturer, contains all this information and more. The FDA requires that the manufacturer give that information to doctors, pharmacists, and anyone who may purchase the product.

But where does the information come from? How can a drug's side effects be predicted? How do manufacturers know what side effects may occur?

Testing for Adverse Reactions

Before a drug, any drug, can be sold in the United States, its manufacturer must prove to the FDA that the drug is both safe and effective for its intended use. To prove its safety and to demonstrate that the drug actually does what it claims to do, drug manufacturers test their drugs in people through a procedure called clinical trials (see chapter two).

Let's say researchers at a fictional pharmaceutical company called Dandy Drug Developers, Inc. (DDD) discover a new drug, called Wonder Cure, that they think will eliminate bipolar disorder. The scientists run tests in the laboratory, the results of which look promising. They test Wonder Cure on lab rats, mice, rabbits, and monkeys to see if it might be safe for other mammals (humans are mammals, too). They observe what effect Wonder Cure has on the animals' organs and how the animals' bodies absorb, use, and get rid of each chemical in the drug. So far, everything looks safe.

After completing this preclinical research (tests done on a drug *before* it is tested in humans), DDD goes to the FDA and says, essentially, "We've developed a new drug called Wonder Cure that we

Common Adverse Reactions and What to Do If They Occur

Adverse Reaction (side effect)	What to Do
All listed below	Most side effects will disappear without doing anything at all if you wait two weeks.
Dry Mouth	Brush and floss your teeth regularly. Suck on sugarless hard candies.
Difficulty sleeping	Exercise early in the day. Avoid caffeine. Go to bed at the same time each night. Do something soothing at bedtime (take a hot bath, read, listen to quiet music). Take your medication in the morning.
Constipation	Add fiber to your diet. Increase your fluid intake.
Cramps, nausea, diarrhea	Use over-the-counter stomach remedies like Pepto-Bismol, or ask your doctor to temporarily lower your medication dosage.
Dizziness	Stand up, change positions, or sit down slowly. Don't drive.
Headaches or decreased sexual desire or function	Ask your doctor to temporarily lower your dosage.

Before the FDA, medications could be sold to the public without any official approval. Many manufacturers made claims for their products that had no basis in reality.

think will help people with bipolar disorder. We've tested Wonder Cure in the lab and on animals, and everything looks good. Here's our research so far. Now we plan to test Wonder Cure on humans."

After looking at DDD's preclinical research results, the FDA can object (if it sees safety issues for testing in humans), or it can allow DDD to proceed. If the FDA doesn't object, DDD can begin testing Wonder Cure in people. These tests done in people are called clinical trials. By law, DDD must keep records of everything that happens to patients during clinical trials, including any complaints of side effects. These records become the basis for information provided in the package insert the manufacturer later supplies. (For a more detailed explanation of how psychiatric drugs are discovered, developed, tested, and approved, see another book in this series, *The FDA and Psychiatric Drugs: How a Drug Is Approved*.)

So Diane's doctor wasn't guessing. He knew that complaints just like hers (nausea, headache, etc.) had been observed in hundreds of patients during clinical trials and that the symptoms disappeared in time without causing lasting harm. To discover this information, though, you can bet that her doctor didn't go rooting through drug packages and their wadded up pieces of paper for the information he needed. Instead, he consulted a book called *The Physicians' Desk Reference* (PDR).

The PDR is a reference book containing the manufacturer's reports on their drugs. The information in the PDR on any drug listed is identical to the drug's package insert. The PDR is essentially a collection of package inserts bound in one handy volume for quick reference. Having all the manufacturers' reports on their drugs available in one book makes it easier for clinicians to learn about the drugs they prescribe and to check for possible side effects or precautions noted about any drug they might prescribe. It provides a manual for how to safely and effectively use old and new drugs.

The PDR isn't just an important resource for doctors. Available at public libraries and local bookstores, the PDR is an essential resource for patients and their families, too—especially if they want to learn about the drugs they might be taking.

After checking Prozac's package insert in the PDR, Diane's doctor recognized that her symptoms were no cause for alarm. Prozac was essentially safe. Or was it?

How Safe Are Today's Psychiatric Drugs?

Diane's experience is, by far, the more typical experience of a young person who is put on psychiatric medications for mood disorders. Yes, she experienced some mild adverse reactions, but the good Prozac did for her outweighed the mild discomfort she experienced while her body adjusted to the drug. Her experience, however, is not everyone's experience.

We started the chapter with three real-life case studies of young people whose experiences were far different than Diane's: Sarah, who lost all sexual desire; Cora, who had trouble with lockjaw, and the fifteen-year-old young man with OCD who killed himself two weeks after starting on an antidepressant. All three of these teens experienced serious adverse reactions. Does that mean that those reactions will happen to you if you take a psychiatric drug?

Severe adverse events are uncommon—but they do happen. However, they are *rare*. In all likelihood they won't happen to you. If you suspect that you are experiencing an adverse reaction, especially a severe adverse event, it's vital that you call your doctor immediately. He may want to change your dosage, change the type of medication you are taking, or take you off psychiatric drugs

Each package of medication at your local pharmacy contains information about side effects and dosage.

altogether. Never stop taking a medication abruptly without speaking with your medical practitioner.

If this happens, if you must go off psychiatric drugs, your mood disorder does not need to go untreated. There are many alternative treatments for mood disorders that can work safely and effectively while you remain drug free.

Alternative practitioners provide "natural" medications to their patients.

Chapter Seven

Alternative and Supplementary Treatments

D o you remember our thirteen-year-old patient, Patrick Weaver, from chapter four? Do you recall what Dr. Reed, the psychiatrist who treated Patrick, recommended for Patrick's depression? Dr. Reed put Patrick on an antidepressant medication (an SSRI called Zoloft), but he also suggested something else: exercise (Patrick returning to his soccer team) and psychotherapy (meeting weekly with Dr. Reed to talk about what Patrick was thinking and feeling).

In Patrick's case, exercise and psychotherapy would be considered supplementary treatments. Supplementary treatments are treatment strategies doctors or mental health professionals

Question: Where can I find a good therapist?

Answer: There are several places you can go to find out about possible therapists:

- Ask your family doctor to recommend someone.
- Ask your pastor, rabbi, priest, youth worker, or other religious leader.
- Ask your school guidance counselor.
- Call a mental health crisis line.
- Check with your local hospital or clinic.
- Ask friends or family members.
- Talk to other teens.

recommend in *addition* to drug treatment. A patient's drug treatment and supplementary treatments happen at the same time.

What are some common supplementary treatments doctors prescribe for patients with mood disorders? The most common is psychotherapy. In most cases, doctors recommend that drug treatment not be used alone but in conjunction with psychotherapy or counseling: the two go hand in hand.

Psychotherapy

We often call psychotherapy "counseling" or "talk therapy." It is a form of mental health help that involves talking with a psychiatrist, psychologist, advanced practice psychiatric nurse, social worker, therapist, or counselor to work through problems, resolve conflicts, and learn ways of coping with stress or difficult emotions. The differences between psychotherapies are their goals and how long it takes to achieve them.

Cognitive Therapy

This is a type of psychotherapy that tries to help patients replace negative thoughts with positive ones. It focuses on helping someone with a mood disorder learn how to *think* differently. It teaches patients how to tell themselves good things in their minds. Instead of thinking, *I never do anything right,* the patient might tell himself to think: *Well, you might not have done the best job on this one thing, but look at all the other things you do well.* Patients can usually respond to this kind of therapy in a fairly short time.

Behavioral Therapy

This form of therapy focuses on helping patients change the way they behave. It equips the patient to act in ways that will make her feel more fulfilled and satisfied, and to help her unlearn old patterns or habits that make her feel worse. Results from behavioral therapy can be both short term and long term.

Interpersonal Therapy

This helps the patient improve relationship and communication skills, resolve conflict, grow in people skills, and deal with unresolved grief. The focus is primarily on how to get along with others in healthy ways. This type of help requires several months of therapy.

Psychodynamic Therapy

A professional who uses this approach examines past issues and experiences that influence how the patient thinks, feels, and acts today. She will tend to focus less on "how to" skills, and more on thoughts and feelings, and the therapy usually lasts longer than other forms of treatment do. Some patients take years to respond to psychodynamic therapy.

Types of Therapists

- Psychiatrist: medical doctor who specializes in treating mental and emotional problems.
- Psychologist: mental health professional, often holding a Ph.D. or other graduate degree in psychology, who has extensive training in mental health issues, counseling skills, testing and evaluation methods, and treatment strategies. Though highly trained, psychologists are not medical doctors and cannot prescribe medication.
- Therapist: mental health worker who may (or may not) be trained in certain types of psychotherapeutic methods. They may or may not hold counseling degrees and are often unregulated.
- Licensed therapist: trained mental health worker who is under the supervision of and accountable to a licensing board (state, federal, organizational, etc.).
- Counselor: someone who is trained to give more generalized advice about life issues. They may or may not hold counseling degrees.
- Pastoral counselor: a minister, pastor, priest, or rabbi who is trained in counseling methods or psychotherapy skills. His or her counsel will include matters of faith.

Supportive Therapies

These are what we often think of as "counseling," and they focus on providing support for a patient by providing counseling relationships where the patient can be listened to and reassured. Professionals in

Things to Think About
When Choosing a Therapist

- Am I comfortable with this therapist?
- Do I think I can trust her?
- Do her credentials (education, background, specialization, etc.) fit my needs?
- Does she have experience with people like me?
- Does she have a good reputation?
- Can she prescribe drug treatment?
- Will she keep our conversations confidential?
- How long does she expect me to be in therapy?
- How often does she think I need to be seen?
- Can she offer regular appointments?
- Can I cancel an appointment if I need to?
- Does she provide an emergency contact number for off-hours?
- How much does she charge?
- Where is her office located (can I get there easily)?
- Is her office suitable (comfortable, clean, neat, soundproof/private enough)?
- Is the receptionist pleasant?

supportive therapies often listen to a patient's current problems and suggest ways to handle them. These relationships can be short term or long term.

Do's and Don'ts of Exercise

- DO check with your doctor before you start an exercise program.
- DON'T assume you can pick up where you left off, if you used to exercise.
- DO pick an exercise you enjoy—one that's fun for you!
- DON'T force yourself to do something you don't enjoy or that feels like work.
- DO start small. Begin with fifteen minutes three times a week.
- DON'T increase too rapidly. Try adding five minutes per session per week until you reach thirty minutes per session. Then add another session to the week.
- DO stretch. Stretching prevents injury.
- DON'T start exercising without warming up first.
- DO find someone to exercise with. You'll be more likely to stick with it.
- DON'T quit, even if you want to. Exercise is vital to your recovery.

Most health professionals today are trained in one or more of these therapies (there are others). But not all mental health workers use all types of therapy. Some use one type of therapy, while others use several at the same or alternating times. Some will start a patient on one kind of therapy, then switch to another. Some treat patients one-on-one; others work with patients in groups. Treatment styles and methods vary.

The decision to use psychotherapy, which type of therapy to use, and how long to pursue it is a decision that needs to be made with your doctor. He knows best what kind of therapy will work and where to find it.

Exercise

Though doctors commonly tell patients on mood disorder drugs to try psychotherapy, it is not the only supplementary treatment available. Doctors almost always recommend exercise, too, because of how exercise impacts the chemicals (especially neurotransmitters) in the brain.

In a study done at Duke University, 156 adults with mild to moderate major depression were given one of three treatment options:

1. exercise for forty-five minutes three times a week, but don't take medication;
2. take an antidepressant, but don't exercise;
3. do both (exercise forty-five minutes three times a week *and* take an antidepressant).

After four months, the people who *only exercised* experienced as much improvement in their depression as the people who only took medication or who did both. After an additional six months, researchers observed that the people who continued to exercise regularly were the least likely to have their depression come back again.

Exercise provides health benefits. It gives us added energy, better sleep, a healthier heart and lungs, improved self-esteem, and reduced irritability. If mood disorders cause low energy, sleep problems, low self-esteem, and increased anger, then exercise seems like the perfect antidote for a person who struggles with one!

As always, it's important to talk to your doctor before you start an exercise program. If she gives you the "thumbs up" to begin, start slowly. Pick an exercise you enjoy that works easily into your daily

Simple sunlight can have a powerful effect on our emotions.

schedule. Shoot for thirty minutes of continuous (not start-and-stop) exercise at least four days a week.

Alternative Therapies

Psychotherapy and exercise are common supplementary treatments for mood disorders. As we said earlier, doctors often recommend that they be used with drug treatment. But not everyone can or wants to take drugs for their mood disorders. What can they do?

People with mood disorders who don't want or can't take psychiatric medicine can try alternative therapies. These are treatments used *instead of drugs*. One of the most common alternative therapies is light therapy.

Light Therapy

Have you ever noticed how different you can feel depending on the weather? On bright, sunny days we often feel hopeful, energetic, and positive. On cloudy, rainy days we tend to feel more tired and glum. Our different moods are often the result of differences in amount of light we receive. In his work *Beyond Prozac*, Dr. Michael J. Norden notes that light affects serotonin levels: more light causes serotonin levels to go up; less light causes them to go down. If low brain serotonin levels cause us to feel more irritable, less energetic, and less able to sleep (all symptoms of depression), then an increase in serotonin levels should bring relief to those symptoms. One way to increase serotonin without drugs is to use light therapy.

Light therapy, or phototherapy as it is sometimes called, involves having a patient sit in front of a specially designed light—not an ordinary light like you find at home; it must be much brighter and more intense. The recommended brightness of a phototherapy light is ten thousand lux—approximately twenty times brighter than your average living room lamp light bulb.

Lights used in light therapy are designed to be easy to use. They often come in the shape of a large rectangular box about two feet long, one foot high, and three inches deep (although new designs include desk lights and visors). High intensity light bulbs are set inside the box behind an opaque screen (called a diffuser) that protects the patient from dangerous ultraviolet rays and glare. The box can be put on a table top as it is or can be attached to a special frame to tilt the light at an angle more like that of the sun's rays.

For light therapy to be effective, the patient must sit close to the box (usually within twenty inches) and spend a regular amount of time in front of it each day (fifteen minutes to two hours). This treatment is especially effective for people who suffer from seasonal affective disorder (SAD), particularly if they start light therapy in the fall and continue it through the winter and early spring.

It's reported that light therapy helps three out of four people with SAD. It is a highly effective therapy with very few side effects (the primary one is eye strain from the light's brightness). Light therapy is a safe alternative to drug treatment for people with depression (especially SAD), but is also used in combination with drug therapies.

Homeopathic Treatment for Mood Disorders

Homeopathy is a form of alternative medicine that treats disease and disorders from a very different perspective from conventional medicine. It looks at a person's entire physical and mental being, rather than dividing a patient into various symptoms and disorders. Homeopathic medicine uses tiny doses to stimulate the body's ability to heal itself. In some cases, these doses may be administered only once every few months or years.

According to Judyth Reichenberg-Ullman and Robert Ullman, authors of *Prozac Free: Homeopathic Medicine for Depression, Anxiety, and Other Mental and Emotional Problems*, homeopathy offers safe, natural alternatives that can supplement or replace conventional pharmaceutical treatment. They recommend this form of treatment because it has fewer side effects than conventional drugs.

While light therapy is a great alternative, it's not the only choice. Some choose "natural" drugs instead.

Herbs and Vitamins

If you are considering taking herbal or vitamin supplements instead of FDA-approved prescription drugs to treat your mood disorder or its symptoms, remember two things:

1. Herbs and vitamins are chemicals, and chemicals *are* drugs. Any chemical you put into your body can alter the way you think, act, or feel. Just because a chemical takes the form of an herb or vitamin doesn't mean it is not a drug. And, since herbs and vitamins are drugs, they can (and will) cause side effects.
2. Herbs and vitamins are *not* regulated by the FDA. That means that one brand of Saint-John's-wort (an herb often used for

depression) might have far more active ingredients in each pill than another. With "natural" drugs, it's harder to be sure of what you're getting and how much to take. You'll have to watch carefully that you don't take too much.

Let's assume that you're already aware of both facts, but you still want to treat your mood disorder with herbs. As with any drug, you should consult with your doctor first to determine what is right for you. What kind of herbs should you ask your doctor about? Which are most common and what do they do? Here are just a few:

- Saint-John's-wort (also called hypericum perforatum) relieves mild depression.
- Ginkgo biloba improves memory by increasing blood flow to brain.
- Hops has a calming effect and makes you sleepy.
- Kava reduces anxiety.
- Caffeine improves mood.
- Melatonin (a hormone) improves memory and helps you sleep.

Many people with mood disorders, especially Europeans, report being helped by these alternatives. But these substances also cause side effects.

- Saint-John's-wort can cause sensitivity to sunlight, dry mouth, upset stomach, dizziness, and diarrhea.
- Ginkgo biloba can cause upset stomach, dizziness, headaches, and allergic reactions.
- Hops has no side effects.
- Kava, after large doses, can cause muscle spasms, shortness of breath, and yellow skin.
- Caffeine use can lead to addiction, "the jitters," sleep problems, restlessness, while withdrawal from caffeine can cause depressed mood, headaches, and irritability.
- Melatonin can cause light sensitivity.

If you decide to take herbs or vitamins, tell you doctor. As with any drugs these remedies can interact with routine medications (including cold or cough syrups, pain relievers, and allergy medications) and could cause potentially dangerous side effects when taken with other drugs. If you have any doubts or questions, ask your doctor!

Other Alternatives

People with mood disorders have a host of other treatment options from which to choose: diet and dietary supplements (what you eat can affect how you feel); electroconvulsive therapy (ECT; yes, this is still around, but it is a safe, painless treatment today); acupuncture (the ancient Chinese practice of inserting tiny needles into certain pressure points, which is reported to work as well as drug treatment with fewer side effects); aromatherapy (using scented oils to trigger emotional responses); massage therapy (total body massage to cause deep muscle relaxation); and meditation and relaxation techniques.

How to treat your mood disorder is a deeply personal choice, one that should involve you, your family, and a mental health professional. With the number of options available today, you should be able to find a treatment strategy that works for you.

As you begin treatment, remember: you will have good days and bad days. Overcoming a mood disorder takes time. If one treatment option doesn't work, try another. Be flexible. And don't forget to allow loved ones to help you. When they receive love, support, and understanding, along with the proper medical treatment, most people with mood disorders can overcome their disorders, or learn to live successfully with them. In either case, it takes great courage to risk treatment and change. When people with mood disorders are willing to take the risk, and get the help and support they need, they can lead happy, fulfilled lives as the men and women they were intended to be.

Further Reading

Drummond, Edward H. *The Complete Guide to Psychiatric Drugs: Straight Talk for Best Results*. Hoboken, N.J.: John Wiley and Sons, 2006.

Kaufman, Miriam. *Overcoming Teen Depression: A Guide for Parents*. Buffalo, N.Y.: Firefly, 2001.

Kramlinger, Keith. *Mayo Clinic on Depression*. Rochester, Minn.: Mayo Clinic Health Information, 2001.

Miklowitz, David J. *The Bipolar Disorder Survival Guide*. New York: Guilford Press, 2011.

Silverstein, Alvin, Virginia Silverstein, and Laura Silverstein Nunn. *The Depression and Bipolar Disorder Update.* Springfield, N.J.: Enslow, 2008.

Welch, Edward T. *Depression: The Way Up When You Are Down*. Phillipsburg, N.J.: P & R Publishing, 2000.

Wilens, Timothy E. *Straight Talk about Psychiatric Medications for Kids*. New York: The Guilford Press, 2008.

For More Information

American Academy of Child and Adolescent Psychiatry
www.aacap.org

American Foundation for Suicide Prevention
www.afsp.org

Canadian Mental Health Association
www.toronto.cmha.ca

Center for Mental Health Services
www.mentalhealth.org

Depression and Bipolar Support Alliance (DBSA)
(formerly the National Depressive and Manic-Depressive Association [NDMDA])
www.dbsalliance.org

Mood Disorders Association of Manitoba
www.depression.mb.ca

Mood Disorders Association of Ontario (MDAO)
www.mooddisorders.on.ca

National Alliance for the Mentally Ill
www.nami.org

National Foundation for Depressive Illness
www.depression.org

National Institute of Mental Health
www.nimh.nih.gov

National Mental Health Association
www.nmha.org

Stanley Center for the Innovative Treatment of Bipolar Disorder
www.stanleyresearch.org/dnn

Publisher's Note:
The websites listed on these pages were active at the time of publication. The publisher is not responsible for websites that have
changed their address or discontinued operation since the date of
publication. The publisher will review and update the websitesupon
each reprint.

Index

quetiapine (Seroquel) 54

risperidone (Risperdal) 54

seasonal affective disorder (SAD) 13, 21, 26, 49–51, 101, 119
selective serotonin reuptake inhibitors (SSRIs) 37, 39, 45, 47, 63, 78, 99, 111
serotonin 37, 45, 53, 60–61, 63, 66, 119
sertraline (Zoloft) 47, 54, 60, 75, 78–79, 82–83, 111
substance-induced mood disorder 30

topiramate (Topamax) 54
treatment plans 7–8, 31, 64, 74, 78–79

tricyclic antidepressants (TCAs) 37, 39, 43–44, 47

U.S. Centers for Disease Control and Prevention (CDC) 16
U.S. Food and Drug Administration (FDA) 9, 28, 38–39, 41, 63, 93, 95–97, 100, 103–104, 106–107, 120–121

valproate (Depakote) 54, 78
venlafaxine (Effexor) 54, 60, 75, 78

About the Author & Consultants

Joan Esherick is a full-time author, freelance writer, and professional speaker who lives outside of Philadelphia, Pennsylvania. Joan has contributed dozens of articles to national print periodicals, written spiritual and educational books, and speaks nationwide.

Mary Ann McDonnell, Ph.D., R.N., is the owner of South Shore Psychiatric Services, where she provides psychiatric services to children and adolescents. She has worked as a psychiatric nurse at Franciscan Hospital for Children and has been a clinical instructor for Northeastern University and Boston College advanced-practice nursing students. She was also the director of clinical trials in the pediatric psychopharmacology research unit at Massachusetts General Hospital. Her areas of expertise are bipolar disorder in children and adolescents, ADHD, and depression.

Donald Esherick has worked in regulatory affairs at Rhone-Poulenc Rorer, Wyeth Pharmaceuticals, Pfizer, and Pharmalink Consulting. He specializes in the chemistry section (manufacture and testing) of investigational and marketed drugs.